THE MIXELLANY GUIDE TO VERMOUTH & OTHER APÉRITIFS

THE MIXELLANY GUIDE TO
VERMOUTH
& OTHER APÉRITIFS

JARED BROWN & ANISTATIA MILLER

MIXELLANY LIMITED

Mixellany books may be purchased for educational, business, or sales promotional use. For information, please write to Mixellany Limited, 3 Eyford Cottages, Upper Slaughter, Cheltenham GL54 2JL United Kingdom or email jaredbrown1@mac.com

First edition

ISBN: 978-1-907434-25-9

British Library Cataloguing in Publication Data.
A catalogue record for this book is available from the British Library.

CONTENTS

ACKNOWLEDGEMENTS

[Acknowledgements to come in the final edition.

CHAPTER ONE

WHAT IS VERMOUTH?

We're drinking vermouth as we write this book. We're drinking it chilled, poured straight from bottle to glass. It is delicious. The French know this. So do the Italians. Argentines and Chileans like it so much their cocktail hour is called *l'hora del vermut* [the vermouth hour]. In some regions of Spain bodegas have barrels of vermouth to dole out afterwork aperitivos. And in the cafés you can tell the time by the goblets of vermouth on the rocks. Yet in the United Kingdom and the United States, peoples' understanding of vermouth is still stuck in the days when Chateau Margaux was known as claret.

Winston Churchill allegedly bowed toward France instead of using vermouth. Over the decades various eyedroppers and misters have been marketed to administer minute amounts of this aromatized wine into cocktails. Some barmen pride themselves in simply waving the bottle over the shaker, unless a customer specifically asks for it. The result: Vermouth has been treated as a necessary evil, when in truth it is the most wrongly maligned beverage behind bars today.

If drinking is purely for pleasure, why should any evil be necessary? If vermouth is so awful, why use it at all? The answer is simple. Vermouth is not evil. It is tragically mistreated and misunderstood.

Vermouth is not a spirit. It is, at its foundations, a wine. Imagine that you opened a 1982 Petrus, left it to breathe, then forgot about it for a week. Would you consider drinking it, or even make salad dressing with it? Of course not. You'd make sure no one was looking and quietly pour it down the drain. You might say it is an unfair comparison as vermouth has a higher alcohol content. Petrus contains 14% alcohol, vermouth ranges from around 14% to 18%, which is still less than port. And anyone who understands port knows it only lasts between one (ruby) and four (tawny) months once it has been opened and recorked.

Yet even today, vermouth sits behind many bars in the well, topped with a pour spout, leaving it effectively open and breathing until it is emptied in six, twelve, or eighteen months. Of course you'd rather bow to France than have a splash of stale, vinegary vermouth in your drink.

Handled properly, fresh vermouth brings complexity to a Martini, spice and strength to a Manhattan, softness to an

Americano, richness and balance to all. It is also delicious on its own, and has plenty of character to stand up on the rocks. Few summer drinks are as quenching as equal parts sweet vermouth with freshly squeezed orange juice.

Julia Child, who introduced French cuisine to the United States, was known to enjoy Reverse Martinis, mixing five parts dry vermouth to one part gin in a wine goblet filled with ice. Childs' Reverse Martini inspired the Reverse Manhattan, which paradoxically tastes stronger than a standard Manhattan because the botanicals burst forth amid the headiness of the wood-aged spirit.

Of all concoctions in the vermouth family of drinks the Martini has received the most attention. This is appropriate for two reasons. First, the Martini (especially the Vodka Martini) highlights the vermouth as the spirit's neutrality reveals all of its character unmasked. The Gin Martini is a unique marriage. The vermouth contains many of the botanicals found in most London dry style gins, as well as a host of other complementary herbs and spices.

Few wines pair as well with firm-fleshed fish such as swordfish or halibut than this aromatic apéritif. Of course, vermouth also pairs naturally with any dish in which it is used. Try it in a risotto or osso bucco or roast a chicken basted with lemon, oregano, and dry vermouth.

We have always been fans of vermouth. For me (Jared here), it was the summer of 1976. Sitting beneath a Cinzano umbrella at a dockside restaurant in Upstate New York. The acclaimed chef Georgine Cavaiola ordered a round of vermouth and fresh squeezed orange for the table. Somehow I got my hands on one and was instantly enthralled. For me (Anistatia here) the epiphany first came when I was mixing Martinis for my father, then when he took me for my first Martini outside the home, at the American Bar in London's Savoy Hotel.

But it seems the world doesn't discover vermouth this way anymore. This book was inspired in part by an evening out with two marketing representatives of a major vermouth brand, in a famous bar, in a major city (I would rather not embarrass the parties involved). When their backs were turned, I ordered a straight vermouth and offered it to them to taste. Both loved it. And both admitted they had never tried it straight before. On another evening in the same city, I placed the same order in another downtown cocktail bar. As the young bartender poured it he said, "I could never respect anyone who drinks straight vermouth."

This outstanding apéritif, this essential cocktail ingredient is far more complex to produce than most liqueurs, wines and spirits. It brings more complexity to a drink than most other ingredients. In this book we hope to dispel the myths that it is somehow inferior, secondary and optional in drinks, and of marginal value. It was and continues to be one of the most essential ingredients behind the bar. It appears in innumerable classic cocktails and, as bartenders rediscover vermouth and care for it properly, it is adding its flavour to a new generation of drinks—tomorrow's classics.

The history of vermouth has been told a few times, but with so many additional historical resources available to us today, we have been able to uncover much more and to answer some of the oldest mysteries about the product. For example, why did Italian producers—long presumed to be the inventors—use the German name wermut, or vermouth? The answer is one of many you will find in this book.

While it would be impossible to include every great mixed drink with vermouth, we have attempted to create a comprehensive set of classic recipes, both common and obscure. These should be enough to keep any vermouth lover mixing for some time.

We have also been searching out and tasting rare vermouths as well as the better known ones. It is surprising how many brands and styles of vermouth are produced and consumed in Spain, but not exported. There are new vermouths popping up in some surprising places as well, such as Oregon. And there are new vermouths from Torino [aka: Turin], one of the spiritual homes of vermouth. While we would never claim to have a complete list, we have tried to round up as many as possible for you here.

THE LEGAL JARGON

Vermouths are so cherished in Europe that some have been awarded protected geographical designation status. Similar to the AOC (*appellation d'origine controllée*) qualifications given to wines, protected geographical status sets spirits such as Greek ouzo and Plymouth dry gin apart from copy cats. It does the same for fortified wines. Sherry must legally be made in Spain's Sherry Triangle. Port has to be produced from grapes grown in Portugal's Douro region and processed in the same zone.

And it follows the same suit or some aromatized and/or fortified wine-based drinks. Nürnberger Glühwein [Glow Wine] can only hail from Nuremberg, Germany. Vermouth de Chambéry must be produced in France's Savoy region surrounding the former capital of Chambéry. And Vermouth di Torino can only be made in the Piedmonte region surrounding the northern Italian city of Torino [aka: Turin].

Protection under European Union laws, as of 10 June 1991, assures the consumer that the product—as stated on the label—is manufactured according to specific guidelines and is authentically produced in a specified region. It also protects manufacturers from copycats who might attempt to flood the market with lower-quality, lower-priced knockoffs. In regions where the economy relies on traditional production of such a unique commodity, this distinction ensures communities financial stability as well as continued support of the cultural infrastructure. Globalization has homogenized so much of what is deemed "cultural identity". It is refreshing to know there is a governing body defending the uniqueness of character found in products such as vermouth. Of course there are copycats. But if a vermouth made in the Vermouth di Torino style is not manufactured in that region, it has to be clearly stated on the package.

Compliance with strictly-monitored rules allows producers to maintain this designation. So what does that mean in the case of vermouth and other aromatized drinks?

Council Regulation (EEC) No 1601/91 categorizes aromatized drinks into three subdivisions:

1. aromatized wine or wine-based apéritif
2. aromatized wine-based drink
3. aromatized wine-product cocktail

Sangria, Clarea, Zurra, bitter soda, Kalte Ente, Gluehwein, Maiwein, Maitrank, and the like all fall in the second and third subcategories. However, our focus is on the first distinction—aromatized wine or wine-based apéritif. This family of drinks encompasses far more than vermouth, if you following the European Union's definition.

An aromatized wine or wine-based apéritif is a drink that is based on wines that comply with equally strict cultivation and fermentation guidelines (with the exception of retsina table wine). Wine makes up a minimum of 75% of the total content, with only fresh or fermented grape must and alcohol added to the final liquid. This wine blend can be flavoured with natural flavouring substances and/or preparations, aromatic herbs, spices and/or flavouring foodstuffs. To achieve a consistent end product, sweetening and caramel are also allowed.

Just as it does with Champagne, the level of sweetness also determines whether an aromatized wine can be called sweet or dry. Extra-dry means that the product has less than 80 grams of sugar per litre. Dry signifies that there is less than 50 grams per litre. Semi-dry indicates a sugar content of between 50 and 90 grams per litre. Semi-sweet means there is between 90 and 130 grams of sugar per litre. And Sweet states that more than 130 grams per litre of sugar can be found in the bottle.

In its finished state, an EU-compliant aromatized wine must have an actual alcoholic strength of 14.5% to 22% ABV or more. If the product is intended to be "dry", it must have a minimum total alcohol strength of 16% ABV. "Extra dry" has a minimum set at 15% ABV.

If an aromatized wine does not comply with every single regulation, it cannot be marketed even with such marketing tags as "style", "type", or "flavour".

There are a couple of other things that set aromatized wine apart from its siblings—aromatized wine-based drinks and aromatized wine-product cocktails. The latter are not fortified with additional alcohol. They can contain 50% to 75% wine, and have an actual alcoholic strength of 7% to 14.5% ABV.

This rather broad definition of aromatized wine is further subdivided, focusing on the herbs, spices, and other aromatic elements used in each variety.

THE AROMATIZED WINE FAMILY

The EU is very specific in stating how vermouth is set apart from other aromatized wines. It must contain one of three varieties of wormwood (Artemisia absinthium, Artemisia pontica, or Artemisia maritima). It can only be sweetened with caramelized sugar, sucrose, grape must, rectified concentrated grape must and concentrated grape must. Then there are "bitter aromatized wines" with similar specifications.

Quinquina wine has to contain a quinine flavour component. Gentian is required to be the primary botanical if a product is called *bitter vino*. And the finished liquid must be tinted with EU-approved yellow and/or red colouring. Wormwood and gentian must both be apparent in the character of an Americano, which also has to be tinted with officially sanctioned yellow and/or red tinting agents.

Egg-based aromatized wines are required to contain a minimum of 10 grams of good-quality egg yolk in every litre of the final product as well as more than 200 grams of sugar. In the case of cremovos, the liquid must contain at least 80% Marsala wine. Cremovo zabaiones follow the same proportion, but the egg yolk content cannot fall below 60 grams per litre.

A final word from the EU about the packaging of aromatized wines was handed down in regards to its packaging. Since 1 January 1993, no aromatized wine bottle seal can be covered with a lead-based capsule or foil, according to EU law, even if they are exported outside of the commercial zone.

BY ANY OTHER NAME

But it is vermouth, above all other aromatized wines, that drives the curiosity and imagination of the bartending community and the unswerving admiration of European café patrons. It is this specific aromatized wine and its herbal liqueur relations that we have targeted in this volume. There's more to vermouth than the maceration of botanicals into wine.

Over the centuries vermouth has gone by dozens of names: vermouth, vermout, vermuth, vermut, wermut, wormwood wine, eisel, vin d'absinthe, vino de axenjo, vino d'assenzio, and so on. The recipes differ from era to era, from producer to producer. But there are three elements each formula shares in common follow the European Union's edicts: wine, wormwood, and fortification with spirit. To understand how this relationship sprouted and blossomed, you have to journey through vermouth's amazing history.

CHAPTER TWO
A HISTORY
OF VERMOUTH

WORMWOOD & WINE IN CHINA

Where did it all begin? An astounding discovery was made, in December 2004, when the contents of a few tightly lidded bronze vessels exhumed in China at Anyang and the Changzikou Tomb in Luyi county were analysed by an international team of archaeologists led by Dr Patrick E McGovern from the Museum of Applied Science Center for Archaeology at the University of Pennsylvania Museum of Archaeology and Anthropology in Philadelphia. The vessels were filled with aromatised wine residues. Made from filtered rice or millet wines, each had been macerated with wormwood, chrysanthemum, China fir, elemi, and other herbs and flowers. The finds were dated to the Shang and Western Zhou dynasties (circa 1250-1000 BC) and resemble the chang wines mentioned in a few Shang dynasty oracle-bone inscriptions.

As McGovern wrote in a 2010 article titled "Wines Fit for Kings and the Afterlife": "By Shang Dynasty times, however, herbs were clearly part of an already highly specialized medicinal wine 'industry.' One wine (*chang*) was specifically denoted as herbal wine in the oracle bone inscriptions. Officials in the Shang palace administration were charged with making the beverages, which the king inspected.... Of the possible ingredients and additives identified in the Chang-zikou wine, the two species of Artemisia [probably sweet wormwood (Artemsia annua) or Qing Ho plus common wormwood which is native to Siberia and Manchuria] stood out because of their long-standing importance in Traditional Chinese Medicine up to the present."

Three oracle-bone inscriptions allude to chang wine's place in the king's daily life:

> "...on the hai day. Xi divined:...should use chang wine at the jue wine offering. [Note: Chang wine (aka: black millet wine) is used as an offering to an ancestor, but never to a nature spirit.]

"...on the 53rd day. It was divined: we shall perform the jue wine offering in reporting illness to...in the ding [temple] using new chang wine.

"...Da [divined]...we should use chang wine in performing the jue wine offering to...in the ancestral temple."

From McGovern's current research, it's pretty obvious that chang wine is vermouth's earliest ancestor.

FROM ANCIENT INDIA TO ANCIENT GREECE

Wormwood played a key role in India, where medical principles handed down by oral tradition were outlined around 1500 BC in the Atharvaveda, one of the four Vedas—the first written texts of cumulative Indian knowledge, wisdom, and culture. Ayurvedic herbal wine recipes containing wormwood were prescribed to treat intestinal worms, anaemia, heart conditions, and poor appetite. The botanical also proved to be an effective antibacterial.

Although the Greek physician Hippocrates is credited, around 400 BC, with infusing wormwood into white wine—creating *vinum absinthianum* or Hippocratic wine—it was Pliny the Elder who provided a specific formula. In his 37-volume work *Naturalis Historia* [Natural History], which was written around 77 AD, he extolled the virtues of aromatized wine in medical practice. In Book 14, Chapter 19, the Roman naturalist documented the basic process for making 66 different varieties of "artificial" wine .

He described how to make wormwood wine "made of Pontic wormwood [Artemisia pontica or Roman wormwood] in the proportion of one pound to forty sextarii of must [young wine], which is then boiled down until it is reduced to one third, or else slips of wormwood put in wine." After giving the formula for making hyssop wine, he further remarked that "both of these wines may be made also in another method, by sowing these plants around the roots of vines." The character of wormwood—and equally of hyssop—is so strong that it can impart its bitterness via its roots to neighbouring plants.

Similarly Lucius Junius Moderaturs Columella in his first century masterwork *De Re Rustica* [On Agriculture] provides a recipe for boiling wine with wormwood, reducing it down to a third of its volume to achieve the desired effect.

However, the five-volume *De Materia Medica* by Pedanius Dioscorides, also written during the first century AD, was the one pharmaceutical manual from ancient Greco-Roman time that remained in continuous circulation without censorship by the Church well into the late 1600s. In volume 3, he recommends that *apsinthion* [Artemisia absinthium] "is warming, astringent and digestive, and takes away bilious matter sticking in the stomach and bowels. It is urinary, and keeps one from overindulging taken as a drink beforehand. It is good (taken as a drink with seseli [wild celery] or celtic nardus [Celtic spikenard]) for gaseousness and pains in the intestines and stomach. Three cups of a dilution or decoction of it (taken every day) heals lack of appetite and jaundice." He also noted that wormwood wine was a popular drink in Propontis and Thracia, "which they use in absence of fever... They drink to each other with it to cause health."

This wormwood wine was also the toast handed to the winner of a biennial chariot race that circuited the outskirts of Rome: a prize of health and stimulated appetite rewarded the driver after miles of grueling, dusty driving.

It was Dioscorides' collection of recipes in volume 5 for *Oinos Apsinthites* [Wormwood Wine] that inspired medieval scholars cloistered in Europe's numerous monasteries to de-velop proprietary recipes:

"Some mix one pound of Pontic wormwood with forty eight pints of water and boil it until a third is left. Afterwards they pour on it six pints of must and half a pound of wormwood. Then having mixed them carefully they put it in a jar and strain it out when it is settled. Others put a pound of worm-wood into nine gallons of must, beat it, and binding it in a thin linen cloth, leave it alone for two months. Others put three or four ounces of wormwood and two ounces each of Syrian nard, cinnamon, cassia, flowers of juncus odoratus, and Phoenicean dates into nine gallons of must, beat them in a mortar (afterwards corking it tightly) and leave it alone for two or three months. Then it is strained, placed in other jars and stored. Others put fourteen ounces of Celtic nard and forty ounces of wormwood, binding it in a linen cloth, into a measure of must, and after forty days store it in other jars. Others put one pound of wormwood and two ounces of dry pine rosin into twenty pints of must, and after ten days they strain it and put it in jars."

EISEL & ALE

The pharmacological arts transited from monastic hands to secular ones with the dawn of the Renaissance. Johannes Gutenberg's invention, in 1439, of movable type printing in made information more widely available. Thus, word of Wormwood wine and its merits spread across Europe and then to the British Isles, where it was popularly dubbed eisel.

It appears that this eisel was not a beverage with complex and appealing character. Quite the opposite, if you are to believe the inferences of playwright William Shakespeare, who obviously thought that this bitter medicine was just that—a bitter medicine, not the popular toast taken to stimulate the appetite in Dioscorides' ancient Propontis and Thracia.

As Shakespeare's tragic Danish character Hamlet rants in grief over the death of his beloved Ophelia, eisel was a punishment rather than a pleasantry, lamenting that:

> 'Swounds, show me what thou'lt do:
> Woo't weep? woo't fight? woo't fast? woo't tear thyself?
> Woo't drink up eisel? eat a crocodile?
> I'll do't. Dost thou come here to whine?

To outface me with leaping in her grave?
Be buried quick with her, and so will I:
And, if thou prate of mountains, let them throw
Millions of acres on us, till our ground,
Singeing his pate against the burning zone,
Make Ossa like a wart! Nay, an thou'lt mouth,
I'll rant as well as thou.

By 1600, when the Bard's play was written, eisel may have been painful to the palate, but there were alternatives. Brewers had been adding herbs—even the bitter ones such as ground ivy, clary sage, or mugwort—to malted ales to preserve their freshness. The "Water Poet" John Taylor, in his 1618 memoir with the extensive and explicative title *The Pennylesse Pilgrimage; or, the Moneylesse Perambulation of John Taylor, alias the Kings Magesties Water-Poet; How He TRAVAILED on Foot from London to Edenborough in Scotland, Not Carrying any Money To or Fro, Neither Begging, Borrowing, or Asking Meate, Drinke, or Lodging*, described a hospitable reception upon his arrival in Manchester when his host offered:

"... Eight several sorts of ale we had,
All able to make one stark drunk, or mad.

We had at one time set upon the table
Good ale of hyssop ('twas no Aesop fable);
Then we had ale of sage, and ale of malt,

And ale of wormwood that could make one halt;
With ale of rosemary, and bettony,
And two ales more, or else I needs must lie.
But to conclude drinking aley-tale,
We had a sort of ale called scurvy ale."

British diarist and dedicated drinker Samuel Pepys also found wormwood ale appealing. In a diary entry on 19 February 1659 he wrote: "Early in the morning I set my books that I brought home yesterday up in order in my study. Thence forth to Mr Harper's to drink a draft of purle…"

Another name for wormwood ale, purl was an infusion of sea wormwood flowers—and sometimes the addition of orange peel and senna—into beer. (Purl-royal was a slang term for wormwood wine.) Even Shakespeare had made mention of purl in his play *The Merry Wives of Windsor*, but with Pepys it becomes apparent that wormwood-laced drinks had become common and downright trendy.

In an entry dated 10 January 1660 Pepys recalls that: "So we both went forth (calling first to see how Sir [Admiral William] Penn do, whom I found very ill), and at the Hoop by [London] bridge we drank two pints of wormwood and sack." Then on 24 November of the same year he scribed: "...where after I had done talking with him [Sir Edward Montagu, Earl of Sandwich], [Thomas] Townsend, [William] Rumball, [Robert] Blackborne, [John] Creed and Mr Shepley and I went to the Rhenish winehouse [on Kong Street], and there I did give them two quarts of Wormwood wine, and so we broke up." And again on 21 March 1661 he writes that: "Here I met with [James] Chetwind, [Thomas] Parry, and several others, and went to a little house behind the Lords' house to drink some wormwood ale, which doubtless was a bawdy house, the mistress of the house having the look and dress:..."

It's pretty obvious that health and pleasure intersected when it came to brewing and distillation. In less than 200 years, Europeans embraced alcohol, wines, and beers as social refreshments, as dining accompaniments, not just as a clever vehicle for delivering botanicals in a palatable form. British physician Dr John French lived in the era when chemistry evolved from alchemy, especially in the field of medicine.

He avidly pursued distillation as a result. And relying heavily on Hieronymous Brunswig's 1500 book *Liber de arte distillandi; Das buch der rechten kunst zu distillieren*, he published his landmark 1651 volume *The Art of Distillation*.

Volume Two on "Compound Waters and Spirits" clearly demonstrates the culinary finesse that had evolved over the century, especially in his recipe for *Aqua Celestis* [Heavenly Water]:

"Take of cinnamon, cloves, ginger, nutmegs, zedoary, galangal, long pepper, citron pill, spikenard, lignum aloes, cububs, cardamum, calamus aromaticus, germander, ground pine, mace, white frankincense, tormentil, hermodactyls, the pith of dwarf elder, juniper berries, bay berries, the seeds and flowers of motherwort, the seeds of smallage, the seeds of fennel, seeds of anise, the leaves of sorrel, the leaves of sage, the leaves of felwort, rosemary, marjoram, mints, pennyroyal, stechados, the flowers of elder, the flowers of red roses, the flowers of white roses, of the leaves of scabious, rue, the lesser moonwort, agrimony, centory, fumitory, pimpernel, sow thistle, eyebright, maidenhair, endive, red launders, aloes - of each two ounces, pure amber, the best rhubarb—of each two drams, dried figs, raisins of the sun, stoned dates, sweet almonds, grains of the pine—of each an ounce.

"Of the best aqua vitae to the quantity of them all, of the best hard sugar a pound, of white honey half a pound. Then add the root of gentian, flowers of rosemary, pepperwort, the root of briony, sow bread, wormwood— of each half an ounce."

"Now before these are distilled, quench gold being made red hot, oftentimes in the aforesaid water, put therein oriental pearls beaten small an ounce, and then distill it after 24 hours infusion.

"This is a very cordial water, good against faintings and infection."

WINE FROM THE SLEEVE OF HIPPOCRATES

Hippocratic wine (aka: hippocras, ypocras, vpocrate, ipocras, ipocrist, *vinum hippocraticum*) was considered to be the most pleasant digestive aid one could administer for intestinal complaints. Macerating botanicals in wine that was sweetened with sugar or honey made the medicine smoothly go down. Contrary to popular assumption, this cordial wine was not invented by Hippocrates. It is known by this name because it was strained through a conical filter bag called a *manicum Hippocraticum* [sleeve of Hippocrates] that was commonly employed by vintners and apothecaries to sieve botanical material out of the wine. Passing the macerated liquid through the bag three or four times achieved the desired result. There were those who added milk, allowing the mixture to curdle upon contact with the wine and ensuring no particles dripped through the bag. This method would also bleach the colour out of red wine, so a plant dye—turnsole, which was derived from the annual plant crozophora tinctoria—was added to restore the liquid to its original colour.

In Volume Five, French explained how to speed up the maceration process:

> "Take what wine you please, and according as you would have it taste of this or that spice or any other vegetable, of one or more together, you may drop a few drops of the distilled oil of the said spices or vegetables into the wine, and brew well together and you may make in an instant all sorts of hyppocras or other wines. As for example, if you would have wormwood wine, two or three drops of oil of wormwood put into a good Rhenish wine, being well brewed together, will make a wormwood wine exceeding any that you shall meet with all in the Rhenish wine houses."

It's not that John French had made any major breakthroughs with hippocras. The recipe had been bantered around London for some time in verse and prose. Written around the 1460s, John Russell's *The Boke of Nature* contained a rather lengthy poem that detailed the construction of hippocras, which in turn, inspired the documentation of the recipe found in the 1508 book *The Booke of Kervinge and Sewing*:

"Take ginger, pepper, graines, canell, sinamon, sugar and tornsole, than looke ye have five or sixe bags for your ipocras to run in, and a pearch that your renners may ren on, than must ye have sixe peuter basins to stand under your bags, than look your spice be ready, and your ginger well pared or if it be beaten to pouder, than looke your stalkes of sinamon be well coloured and sweete: canell is not so gentle in operation, sinamon, is hotte and dry, graines of paradice be hot and moist, ginger, grains, long pepper ben hot and moist, sinamon, canell and redde wine colouring."

John French's contemporary, British botanist, herbalist, astrologer, and physician Nicholas Culpepper consulted with his "two brothers, Dr Reason and Dr Experience" to cull the material for his 1652 book *The English Physitian*. which saw justification in blending wormwood with less bitter accompaniments. He recommended the following wormwood wine recipe as a result:

"Take of the flowers of Wormwood, Rosemary, and Black Thorn, of each a like quantity, half that quantity of saffron; boil this in Rhenish wine, but put it not in saffron till it is almost boiled. This is the way to keep a man's body in health, appointed by Camerarius, in his book entitled Hortus Medicus, and it is a good one too."

Later, in his chapter titled "Physical Wines", he offered a simpler formula for *vinum absynthitis* or wormwood wine:

"Take a handful of dried Wormwood, for every gallon of Wine, stop it in a vessel close, and so let it remain in steep: so is prepared wine of Rosemary flowers, and Eye-bright. ...It helps cold stomachs, breaks wind, helps the wind cholic, strengthens the stomach, kills worms, and helps the green sickness. ...The best way of taking any of these Wines is, to drink a draught of them every morning. You may, if you find your body old or cold, make Wine of any other herb, the virtues of which you desire; and make it and take it in the same manner. ... Now knowe yee the proportions of your ipocras, than beate your pouders, eache by them selfe, and put them in bladders and hange your bagges sure that no bagge tough other, but let each basinge touch other, let the first basin be of a gallon, and each of the other a pottell, than put in your basin a gallon of red Wine, put these to your pouders, and stire them well, than put them into the firste bage, and let it ren, than put them in the second bagge, than take a peece in your hand and assay if it be stronge of Ginger, and alay it with sinamon, and if it be strong of sinamon, alay it with sugar, and look ye let it ren through six renners, and your ipocras into a close Vessel and keep the receit, for it will serve for sewers, than serve your souvraign with wafers and ipocras."

WERMUT WEIN

Britain was not the only European nation drinking wormwood wine. It was well known that Roman wormwood [artemisia pontica], native to southern Europe, was an excellent tonic and strengthened the stomach. Not as bitter as common wormwood, the British botanist and author Dr John Hill, in his 1756 book *The British Herbal: An History of Plants and Trees, Natives of Britain, Cultivated for use or Raised for Beauty*, noted that Roman wormwood is the "most delicate, but least of strength. The Wormwood Wine, so famous with the Germans, is made with Roman wormwood, put into the juice and work'd with it; it is a strong and an excellent wine, not unpleasant, yet of such efficacy to give an appetite that the Germans drink a glass with every other mouthful, and that way eat for hours together, without sickness or indigestion."

Londoners seemed to appreciate the wormwood wine made with the Rhenish wines produced in Germany's Rhine region from Riesling and Silvaner grapes. By all accounts from Pepys, Rhenish wine houses were an alternative to taverns throughout the city. But what of the Wermut Wein made and served back in Germany?

A major figure of the Thirty Years' War (1618-1648), the supreme commander of the Holy Roman Empire's armies provides a glimpse as to the stature of Wermut Wein on the dining tables of German royalty. Albrecht Wenzel Eusebius von Wallenstein was recalled from the battlefield, in 1630, by Emperor Ferdinand II, who suspected that this ambitious military figure was planning a coup to take control of the vast empire that encompassed Germany, Austria, the Czech Republic, Switzerland, Lichtenstein, the Netherlands, Belgium, Luxembourg, Slovenia, portions of eastern France, northern Italy, and western Poland.

Wallenstein sent letters to Gerhard von Taxis, the Captain-General of Friedland, instructing him on various preparations for his return to his dukedom—the Duchy of Friedland in northern Bohemia. He regularly sent reminders that "sweet-smelling blue violets" were to be placed daily in his wife Isabella von Harrach's retiring-rooms at their palace in Gitschin. But in one obviously happy letter he wrote: "Make provision of all things against my coming, especially of new wine...have good Wormwood wine prepared also, both sweet and dry...Let all the stables in Gitschin be made ready, and the riding-school and the tennis-court... It would be well that you and the Master of the Fabric should attend me in Prague...Bid the Game-Warden have the toils in good order, for when I come I wish boar-hunts to be held; let him order whatever may be necessary."

Wermut wein was not the only style of aromatized wine traditionally produced throughout the Holy Roman Empire. Rhenish wine macerated with sweet woodruff called Maitrank [May wine] was served on May Day. A common sight during Christmas in Nüremburg, Gluehwein [Glow Wine] married rich, red wine with lemon, cardamom, clove, bay leaf, and cinnamon, which was served hot—sometimes with a touch of kirschwasser as fortification. What better way to preserve the strength of the botanicals as well as the sweetness of the wine.

THE FORTIFYING TOUCH

Fortification or mutage is a process frequently applied in the production of Champagne, Port, Sherry, vin du naturel, and vermouth. So who came up with the inspiration of retarding the natural fermentation that occurs in wine by adding a small portion of distilled spirit?

We can thank Arnaud de Villeneuve. Both Spain and France claim de Villeneuve as a native son. The Spanish say he was born in the Catalan village of Villaneuva, while the French declare his birthplace was Villeneuve-Loubet near Nice. He is known in both countries by a myriad of other names and spellings: Arnaldus de Villa Nova, Arnaldus de Villanueva, Arnaldus Villanovanus, Arnaud de Ville-Neuve, and Arnau de Vilanova.

What is known of his early life is that he began his education in Barcelona under the tutelage of John Casamila, a celebrated professor of medicine. There, he became attracted to the discoveries of distillation pioneers Claudius Galen (129-216 AD) and al-Razi (865-925 AD).

At the height of his career de Villeneuve was regarded as the best physician and alchemist of his day. He attended to the health of popes Innocent V, Boniface VIII, Benedict IX, and Clement V as well as monarchs Pedro III and James II of Aragon, Robert of Naples, and Frederick II of Sicily. He even served as vice-chancellor At the University of Montpellier whilst teaching medicine, botany, and general alchemy. It was while he was at Montpellier that he and Ramon Llull (the man who first applied the term "alcohol" to potable distillates) experimented with distillation, creating a still designed upon the al-ambiq that was used by Arab alchemists back in the 700s.

ARNALDVS — VILLANOVANVS —

In his 1310 book, *Liber de Vinis* [The Book of Wine], de Ville-Neuve documented his method for distilling wine with his alembic. He termed the result *aqua vine* [water of wine] but noted that: "...some name it *aqua vitae* [water of life] and this name is remarkably suitable since it is really a water of immortality. Its virtues are beginning to be recognised, it prolongs life, clears away ill-humours, revives the heart, and maintains youth."

His excitement over such a miraculous discovery was obvious. Yet it proved to be appropriate a couple of centuries later. *Liber de Vinis* was a best seller and the term *aqua vitae* stuck. (In this same tome, he also advised readers that the optimal circumstance for tasting wine was: "... in the morning after they have rinsed their mouths and eaten three or four bites of bread dipped in water." Again, he was right; the taste buds are highly sensitive in the morning, especially before toothpaste and coffee overwhelm them.)

De Villeneuve's discovery that adding spirits to unfinished wine prematurely arrests fermentation and preserves the liquid's natural sweetness led to the birth of vin doux naturel.

What we now know is that yeast ceases to convert the grape sugars into alcohol when the alcohol level in its environment reaches between 13% and 15%. Stopping fermentation means more sugars are left in the wine. Grape varieties such as Muscat and Grenache are known for their sweetness. Preserving that element increased their popularity as a base for wine. Today, vins doux naturels such as Muscat de Riversaltes, Banyuls, and Maury are still produced and commonly enjoyed in the Languedoc-Roussillon region and its capital, Montpellier.

Aromatized wine had taken a long route across China through Europe, transforming itself from a medicine to a popular drink. Until the late 1500s, only nobility and the aristocracy could afford spices imported from Asia. Only they had the expendable income to serve these botanically-rich digestive aids to guests in a post-prandial ritual that became known as the "void" or issue de table—wormwood wine or hippocras accompanied by thin wafers and comfits.

King William of Orange, England's only Dutch king is remembered for launching gin production in England. His personal physician, Walter Harris, traveled to Holland with him and wrote a book in 1699 titled: *A Description of the King's Royal Gardens at Loo: Together with a Short Account of Holland*. In it, he described the food and drink he encountered on Dutch tables. One drink he did not encounter was jenever. It was presumably still a medicinal relegated to pharmacies and wherever people kept their medications before the invention of bathroom cabinets. Instead, he documented a surprising trend: "They have also every where their Wormwood-wine, which is commonly called by the Name of Alsom Wine, and by the English for sound sake Wholesome Wine, and the which they do not drink only for a Whet before Dinner, or on Physical accounts, but indifferently at any time of the Day, or Evening. It is made of the French Wine before-mentioned, and by its Bitterness does take off that lusciousness, or nauseous taste to Strangers."

Wormwood wine was considered passé, by the mid-1700s, amongst British trendsetters. But in Italy, something magical took place that elevated wormwood wine to becoming the toast of café society.

NATURAL MAGIC

It seems that every Asian and European alchemist of any note wrote a book of secrets, documenting personal revelations on how compounds are made from perfume, incense, cosmetics, incense, medicine, you name it. Each book was, at its core, a practical manual containing tips and tricks discovered by the author to produce their specialties in a more efficient manner.

During the height of the Renaissance, the Chinese, Indian, Greco-Roman, and Arabian secrets of science and medicine—censored by the Church since the 1100s—were being discovered in the secular world. Girolamo Ruscelli authored the findings of one Neopolitan "academy of secrets", of which he was a member, that was founded in the 1540s and dedicated to researching the truth of "natural magic"—the science behind the natural and technological worlds. He had a pseudonym, Alessio di Piemonte. A decade later, in 1555, he published his research in a work titled *I Secreti del reverendo donno Alessio Piemontese* [The Secrets of Alessio of Piedmonte]. It was a best seller, published in Italian and translated into French within a decade. By the 1790s, more than a hundred editions had been reprinted. Within its pages Alessio recorded multiple variations for Hippocras, including a few recipes that called for the wine to be fortified with "ardent water" [spirit].

Much in the same way that demand for Dr Sylvius de la Bouve's juniper-based kidney tonic launched the commercial production and distribution of his discovery, Alessio found himself manufacturing his aromatized wines whilst residing in Venice which, by that time, was a major spice importation hub. Naturally, when a new product reaches a certain level of popularity imitators and imitations quickly follow. And follow they did, especially in the region surrounding Genoa—the rival spice trade port in the Duchy of Savoy's Piemonte region, which stretched from Lake Geneva to Monaco and from Chambéry, France to Pavia, Italy.

Emmanuel Philibert, Duke of Savoy, had designated Torino as the region's capital, in 1563, moving the political seat from its original location in Chambéry and replaced the duchy's official language—Latin—with Italian. Affluent and influential, the city was also home to a large middle class who could afford all of the new, exotic, and inventive items that arrived within its walls.

Aromatized and fortified wines such as those marketed by Alessio were locally produced and gained strong patronage not only because of the city's lavish, expendable income. The Duchy of Savoy was blessed with a rich array of aromatic, alpine botanicals as well as proximity to the Genoese spice trade. Herbal shops dispensed this cornucopia of local and exotic plants not only for medicinal purposes but for culinary pursuits as well. Liqueurs—the fashionable after-dinner drink—and aromatized wines were as integral to a family's closely guarded recipe collection as the perfect truffle risotto or zabaglione formula. Rosolio, a liqueur made with rose petals, was a particular favourite of the Duchal household. An aromatized wine recipe hailing from the foothills to the north was called *Elisir di giovinezza* [Elixir of Youth]. In 700 ml spirit, a mixture of botanicals was steeped for 30 days, including 30 gr Roman wormwood flowers, 20 grams gentian root, 20 grams knapweed, 20 gr bitter orange peel, 15 gr rhubarb, 3 gr China aloes. After the mixture was strained, a pint of white wine was added for bottling.

The Duchy was doubly blessed by its grapes. Along its alpine slopes, vineyards grew an abundant harvest of fragrant Moscato [Muscat], Trebbianno, and Malvasia grapes. Moscato was fermented into sparkling wines such as Asti spumante and Moscato d'Asti, into dessert wine like Vin Santo, and into the new aromatized wines that followed the guidelines set out by Alessio di Piemonte.

FOR THE LOVE OF GOETHE

A product of the city's wealth and stature, café culture was born in Torino. Citizens from all walks of life, from aristocrats to road workers, found time to gather in Torino's ornate caffés, and at tables in front of them under the seventeen kilometres of covered walkways in the city centre. Opened in 1763, the pocket-sized Caffé al Bicerin was one of the first of many establishments that served up familiar refreshments such as morning bavareisa [coffee, chocolate, and milk] or its proprietary, layered version, bicerin.

Aperitvo—between the hours between 6 and 9 PM—was born here as well. It was a social ritual, a time for drinks and *stuzzichini* [appetizers] that demarcated the end of the workday and a prelude dinner. Aperitivo became the time to socialize, to discuss and debate the day in business, finance, politics, arts, literature, sports, religion. The atmosphere was ripe for experiencing and sharing new taste sensations—a new liqueur, a new amaro, a new aromatized wine. If Torino's fashionable café society embraced a new taste, word would rapidly spread across the dukedom.

During the 1780s, Signor Marendazzo owned a wine shop in the heart of Torino: on Piazza della Fiera (now called Piazza Castello) at the corner of Via della Palma (now Via Giovanni Battista Viotti). The piazza was the power base of the Duchy of Savoy, the location of the Palazzo Reale [Royal Palace] and the Palazzo Madama [Madam's Palace after an early resident Regent Marie Jeanne of Savoy]. With such close proximity to an elite clientele and such high demand for his products Marendazzo hired an assistant, Antonio Benedetto Carpano.

Born in 1765, in the municipality of Bioglio Biellese located about 70 km northeast of the capital, Carpano may have gotten his first taste of aromatized wines in this hillside community that was also the home of four monasteries. Maybe the ambitious young apprentice learnt his family's secret to making their home formula for wormwood wine before moving to Torino to make his way in the world. (As mentioned before, it was not uncommon for families living in the dukedom to create their own speciality liqueurs—such as the local ratafia de andorno, made from black cherries—and aromatized wines made from local sweet Erbaluce and lightly bitter Bramaterra wines.

However he first divined, in 1786, his particular blend of 30 botanicals macerated into sweet, floral Moscato wine, his experiment met his employer's approval. Marendazzo allowed the 21-year-old Carpano to sell it in the shop. Having the Duchal household in the same piazza didn't hurt marketing of the product. Lore tells us that a basket of Carpano's Wormwood Wine was sent to Duke Vittorio Amedeo III, who found it so exquisite he suspended his annual order for Rosolio in favour of this new beverage.

There is a romantic story that narrates Carpano's passion for German poetry, especially the works of Goethe. According to this tale, Carpano named his product "wermut", which is the German term for wormwood. What is more likely is that Carpano and Marendazzo wanted to appeal to the Duchal household's close connection with the Holy Roman Empire. Rather than using the local term *vino d'assenzio* or a romantic tag like *elisir di giovinezza* [Elixir of Youth], they employed the German moniker, wermut.

Duchal apppoval naturally created a buzz around the the city about Carpano's fabulous new drink. Ladies in particular found the sweet, complex character of Carpano's vermouth. Wormwood wine finally took a giant leap from being a private production commodity to a becoming commercial product. Intelligent marketing immediately followed.

Cafés cropped up around the piazza as café culture exploded in the vibrant capital, each with its signature drink for aperitivo service. Opened in 1780, Caffé dei Fratelli Fiorio, the "café of the Machiavellis and of the pigtails", was already a fashionable hotbed for artists, intellectuals, and politcians on nearby Via Po. Marendazzo's wine shop was converted into a café that that served patrons 24/7 with vermouth as its show stopper. Eventually, Carpano purchased the business from his employer.

THE ROAD OF GOLD

Another family recipe for wormwood wine made waves in the area around the same time. The Cinzano family had its roots in the village of Pecetto, in foothills near Torino. The family name was linked to the beverage business beginning with Antonio Cinzano, who in January 1568, married Margherita. Their wedding registration entry listed him as a property owner and "producer of elixirs". The area was famed for its cherry harvests and producers like Cinzano made a good living manufacturing fruit eaux-de-vie and ratafias from this bounty.

This tradition was handed down through subsequent generations. According to historian Ernesto Caballo, a 1707 document issued by the Fermieri Generale granted the Cinzano family a royal warrant (*Appaltatori di si Sua Altezza Reale*) to distill eaux-de-vie strictly for sale to the Duchal families residing in Pecetto and Torino.

Duke Carl Emmanuele III established a number of liveries or professional guilds to oversee the quality of goods and services provided by trades such as carriage makers and saddlers. He also granted a livery on 1 August 1739 to the Piemonte's confectioners and distillers, the "University of

Confectioners and Spirits Manufacturers". And it is to this livery that brothers Carl Stefano Cinzano and Giovanni Giacomo Cinzano, were invested as master distillers on 6 January 1757. With these rigorous qualifications in their pockets, they opened a small laboratory and shop in Pecetto and became very active within the guild itself. Carl Stefano was elected, in 1765, as a councilman and four years later became the livery's director.

Giovanni's son Carlo Giuseppe, born in 1755, soon followed in his father's and uncle's footsteps, continuing the family's Pecetto-based distillation business. It is his son, Francisco, born in 1787, who moved the company to Torino, the year after Carpano's death in 1815, opening a shop on the via Dora Grossa (now via Garibaldi) that sold the family's eaux-de-vie and liqueurs and another product. Now that Carpano was dead, Francisco was able to take a major market share by producing and selling the city's favourite aperitivo beverage—vermouth. Then Francisco hired agents to distribute his vermouth across the Duchy of Savoy, stretching his influence from Italy into France.

WINE OF THE FOUR THIEVES

A fabulous fable was handed down throughout southern France about a concoction that was intended to ward off the plague. The story was handed down by oral tradition, so no one can be certain about the exact details. However, it is still worth mentioning. It claims that the merchant ship Grans-Saint-Antoine departed Lebanon laden with silk, cotton, and spices, in 1720, stopping at Smyrna, Tripoli, and plague-ridden Cyprus, en route to iits port of call—Marseille. After a passenger, a few crew members, and the ship's surgeon died from the plague, the ship was refused entry at Livorno. And when it arrived at Marseille, it was immediately quarantined.

The city's powerful merchants pressured authorities and the ban was lifted. A few days later, the Great Plague of Marseille swept through the city before stretching its reach to Aix-en-Provence, Arles, and Toulon. With half of Marseille lying dead in the streets and the other half too weak or scared to act, a band of thieves plundered the abandoned homes and shops immunized by a concoction that William Lewis mentioned in his 1753 book *The New Dispensatory* and George William Septimus Piesse documented in his 1857 book *The Art of Perfumery*: "Take the tops of common wormwood, Roman wormwood, rosemary, sage, mint, and rue of each 3/4 ounce, lavender flowers 1 ounce, garlic, calamus aromaticus, cinnamon, cloves and nutmeg each 1 drachm, camphor 1 ounce, alcohol or brandy 1 ounce, strong 'plonk' [or vinegar] 4 pints. Digest all the materials except the camphor and spirit in a closely covered vessel for fourteen days at summer heat; then express and filter the wine produced and add camphor previously dissolved in brandy or spirit. " Called the "Four Thieves Wine" or "Four Thieves Vinegar", this recipe for an aromatized wine remains a local beverage well into current day.

Across the Camargue and into Languedoc-Roussillon's coastal region, the wines made by local vintners were not highly rated, especially after transport. A Lyonnaise absinthe and liqueur maker named Joseph Noilly enjoyed the taste of Clairette de Languedoc and others of its kind, and he saw their potential. He was intrigued by the distinctive effect that the intense Languedoc sun and Mediterranean salt spray had on the base wines that he shipped down the Canal du Midi to Marseillan, Hérault, the small fishing village where he set up production. Knowing the growing popularity of Vermouth di Torino as well as the Wine of the Four Thieves, he experimented with the creation of a vermouth, applying his expertise with bitter botanicals to the local sea-and-heat caressed wines. Noilly perfected, in 1813, a recipe for a dry style of vermouth, which met with favourable response.

Noilly's son Louis took over the business, in 1829, re-naming it Louis Noilly & Sons. Exportation of its absinthe, liqueurs, and vermouth outside of France commenced the following year. When Louis' brother-in-law Claudius Prat joined the firm, in 1843, it was renamed Noilly-Prat. The next year, the company shipped its products across the Atlantic to the United States, to New Orleans and New York according to surviving paperwork. Business grew to such a point that the vermouth and absinthe bottling operations as well as the firm's management offices were moved to the city of Marseilles while its liqueur production was moved to Lyon.

The only vermouth to be granted an *Appellation d'Origine Controllée* (AOC), which it received in 1932, was born shortly after Noilly began to market his product. Joseph Chavasse developed Dolin Vermouth de Chambéry, in 1821, using local alpine botanicals found in the Rhône-Alpes region of southeastern France. Besides producing dry and sweet varieties, the company created the world's first clear vermouth, vermouth blanc, as well as one that was flavoured with *fraises des bois* [alpine strawberries], Chambéryzette. It is interesting to note, at the time Dolin was invented, Chambéry was part of Sardinia not France, and was ruled from Torino by the same crown that governed the Turinese vermouth producers.

MARKETING TO THE WORLD

The development and expansion of Noilly's and Chavasse's vermouth business did not please King Carlo Alberto of Savoy at all. He was rightfully proud of what his local subjects' companies, Carpano, Cinzano, and others had accomplished in perfecting and producing Vermouth di Torino. Yet until the threat from these competitors made him see the light of day, Torino vermouth producers were not allowed to sell their product outside the city limits.

Giuseppe and Luigi Cora had purchased a small production company owned by Giovanni Rovere, on 30 May 1835, and registered the company Soietà G & L Fratelli Cora. Because of the strong emigration outflux to the United States and South America, the brothers pursued exportation of their vermouth di Torino, in 1838, to supply homesick expats. They also pursued local business, relocating their shop to the Piazza San Carlo.

With this move, Carlo Alberto saw the wisdom to protect his subjects from foreign copycats. And in 1840, he issued licences to protect trade in Vermouth di Torino. There was one other company to enter the playing field that would change the global view of Vermouth di Torino well into the next century.

In the wake of the 1851 Great Exhibition in London, the 1853 Exhibition of the Industry of All Nations held in New York City waved the nationalistic flag on the American side. Within the majestic halls of the New York Crystal Palace, Vermouth di Torino was represented by three producers: G&L Cora, Carpano, and Dettone Brothers.

SLIPS OF PAPER

Distilleria Nazioale de Spirito de Vino had a vermouth production division, in 1849, that was headed by Carlo Re. Located in San Salvatore Monferrato, the company partners lived in Torino. That year, he asked Michael, Agnelli, and Baudino to ship some necessary equipment for production as well as "slips of paper" for labelling the finished bottles.

By the 1860s, production had moved to Pessione and the company needed an injection of fresh blood to move it into the future. The answer came from within the firm itself. Company director Alessandro Martini, vintner Luigi Rossi, and accountant Teofilo Sola, who took over the firm, in 1863, and renamed it Martini, Sola & Cia.

At first, they didn't mark their Vermouth di Torino with "slips of paper"'''' per se. They affixed a die-cut label on the bottle shoulder that bore the authentication "Stabilimento in Pessione" and the company address: Via Carlo Alberto 34, Torino. Pessione was a desirable location for production. On the Torino-Genoa railway line, the company had quick access to spice importation and product exportation to the rest of the world. But by 1864, a "slip of paper" accompanied the shoulder label that boldly presented the company's and product's details, illustrated with Torino's coat of arms set against a backdrop of Italian flags.

The receipt of medals at both the 1865 Dublin International Exhibition and the 1867 Paris International Exhibition that were proudly displayed along with the inscription "By appointment to H.R.M., King Italy [Vittorio Emmanuele II]" when, in 1868, a shipment of champagne-style bottles of the company "vermouth wine" first hit American shores.

Cora now had competition for the North and South American markets for Vermouth di Torino. (They had, in truth, focused their marketing on a local level in direct competition with Carpano, opening the Caffé Monviso on Piazza Venezia, a social spot for members of the liberal Risorgimento [Italian National Unification]).

Although Gancia, founded in 1850 by Carlo Gancia, had entered the vermouth market, it actually concentrated its domestic and export efforts on the production of spumante [sparkling wine] of which they are reputedly the regional originators.

No matter how many copycats and competing producers vied for market share in the global playing field outside of Torino and Marseillan, the development of the vermouth family of cocktails in the United States, United Kingdom, and France would never have occurred without the incredible market savvy of two companies. That story will continue later in the cocktails chapter.

CHAPTER THREE

HOW VERMOUTH IS MADE

You might expect vermouth formulas to be as legendarily guarded as Chartreuse or Angostura Bitters. However, a visit to Noilly Prat in Marseillan, France or Martini and Rossi in Pessione, Italy, includes a comprehensive tour of their herbs and spices. The formulas are well protected by the sheer number of ingredients, their proportions, the unique equipment, and the skill required to marry them during the lengthy production process.

Wine selection is the first, most important step to making a quality vermouth. Without a high-quality base, no amount of botanicals can make up for a poor foundation. There are a few grape varietals employed by the major vermouth producers that are also used in the production of other wines and spirits. Taking a peek at each type provides key insight as to wine's prominence in the making of vermouth.

A GRAPE FOUNDATION

CLAIRETTE: Clairette Blanche yields a high alcohol, low acid wine that easily oxidizes. It is an old domestic grape varietal grown in France's Languedoc region. Clairette overcomes its obvious handicap when it is blended with high acid varietals such as Picquepoul Blanc: the blend that is used to produce Noilly-Prat vermouths. But it is also found in many appellations produced in Languedoc, Provence, and the southern Rhône. One of the thirteen grape varieties permitted in the Châteauneuf-du-Pape appellation and the most common ahead of Grenache Blanc, Clairette is the sole grape in Clairette de Bellegarde and Clairette du Languedoc. In Clairette de Die, a sparkling wine, the grape is blended with Muscat Blanc à Petits Grains.

COLOMBARD: Traditionally grown in France's Charentes and Gascony regions, Colombard plays a primary role in the distilling of some Cognacs and Armagnacs. It also appears in some Bordeaux and Floc de Gascogne wines. Known in North America as French Colombard, this acidic grape is fermented into both dry and sweet versions that bear a distinctive character and is used in making Vya vermouths.

COLOMBOARD, FRENCH: (See Colombard.)

MACABEO: This white grape makes an appearance in Spain's Rioja region and in the cava producing areas south of Barcelona. But Macabeo or Macabeu is also grown in France's Languedoc-Roussillon, where it is picked late and made into vin du naturel. Also known as Viura, this variety yields a mildly acidic wine that is at its best when young. Sometimes it is blended with small amounts of Tempranillo and Garnacha because of its light character. However, it is traditionally blended with Parellada and Xarel-lo to produce sparkling cava. And it is used to make the base spirit for Obsello Absinthe Verte as well as Vermouth Perucci Gran Reserva.

MACABEAU: (See Macabeo.)

MOSCATO: (See Muscat.)

MUSCAT: The sweet character and floral aroma that are distinctively Moscato is what legend tells us Antonio Benedetto Carpano decided to use as the foundation of his vermouth. It is known by many names: Muscat Blanc à Petits

Grains (also called Muscat Blanc, Muscat Canelli, Muscat Frontignan, Moscato Bianco, Muscat de Frontignan, Muscat d'Alsace, Muskateller, Moscatel de Grano Menudo, Moscatel Rosé, Muscat Lunel, Sárgamuskotály, Moscatell de gra petit, Yellow Muscat). Besides Carpano Antique Vermouth, Mocasto can be found in asti, clairette de die, and muscat de Beaumes-de-Venise as well as some Tokaji wines.

MUSCAT: ORANGE: A popular grape that is used to make dessert wines in both California and Australia, Orange Muscat bears the same characteristics as Muscat with a unique difference—it portrays a faint orange aroma. This grape appears in Vya vermouths.

PARALLEDA: One of the three traditional grapes used to make cava (Catalan sparkling wine), Parellada, has a freshness and acidity that also make it a key grape for the production of Vermouth Perucci Gran Reserva as well as for the distillation of Obsello Absinthe Verte.

PICPOUL: Piquepoul or picpoul [meaning "lipstinger"] is one of the oldest domestic grape varities found in France's Languedoc region, along with Cinsaut and Clairette. The grape earned a strong reputation as early as the 1600s for its high acidity. Blended with Clairette, Piquepoul yields the base for Picardan as well as Noilly-Prat vermouths.

PICQUEPOUL: (See Picpoul.)

TEMPRANILLO: The main grape used to make full-bodied Rioja wines, Tempranillo is called the "noble grape". It is Spain's native black grape. Producing a rich, ruby hue and a spicy, herbaceous aroma, this grape imparts a berry character with hints of vanilla and tobacco. Grown in California, this grape is also known as Valdepenas and is used in making Vya Vermouths.

TREBBIANO: The world's second most widely planted grape, you may know Trebbiano by its other name, Ugni Blanc. Fresh and fruity, the high-yielding Trebbiano produces a high-acid wine with a short life. But this structure makes it a prominent element in the production of Cognac, Armagnac, balsamic vinegar, and Cinzano vermouths. Accounting for a third of Italy's white wine production, Trebbiano appears is more than 80 DOCs [Denominations of Controlled Origin] in that nation, including the Orvietos from Umbria. Only six of DOCs bears the Trebbiano name: Trebbiano d'Abruzzo, Trebbiano di Aprilia, Trebbiano di Arborea, Trebbiano di Capriano del Colle, Trebbiano di Romagna and Trebbiano Val Trebbia dei Colli Piacentini. (See also Ugni Blanc)

UGNI BLANC: In all of France, Ugni Blanc is the most widely planted, especially along the coast of Provence as well as in Gironde and Charente. This Floral, aromatic, spicy grape represents 55% of those used in Armagnac production. It is also the grape that serves as the basis for Dolin vermouths. Going by the name Trebbiano, in Italy, this grape is also known as Clairette Ronde, Clairette de Vence, Queue de Renard, St Émilion, and Rossola. (See also Trebbiano.)

VALDEPENAS: (See Tempranillo.)

VIURA: (See Macabeo.)

XAREL-LO: Along with Macabeo and Parellada, Xarel-lo is a Catalan white grape that possesses a strong character and is more aromatic than its counterparts. Used in the production of cava, this grape also appears in Vermouth Perucci Gran Reserva.

Pressed into must—a combination of juice and skins—and fermented with a selected yeast, the wine made from any of these grape varietals is ready to encounter an awe-inspiring harvest of botanicals.

THE GARDEN OF BOTANICAL DELIGHTS

Peeking into the well-documented past of both worm-wood wine and its successor vermouth as they journeyed from China across the Silk Route into Italy and France, it becomes apparent that in each region, in each culture, there are local and exotic botanicals whose significance reaches far beyond the many and varied recipes for aromatized wines. These plants, their native origins, and their essential characteristics are not the only points of interest in a stroll through this aromatic garden: Each botanical is further valued for its historic medical and culinary merits as well as its inclusion in the production of other potables.

ALLSPICE: (Jamaica pepper, Pimenta; Latin: Pimenta dioica) The berries of the allspice tree, a native of Central America's Greater Antilles, were called allspice by the British, around 1621, when they first encountered its warm character. Herbalists administer this spice to relieve indigestion and flatulence. With a complex flavour reminiscent of cinnamon, nutmeg, and clove, the sun-dried berries are found in cuisines that span the globe: from Caribbean jerk seasoning to Near Eastern meat dishes to European sausages and British cakes. In the West Indies, this strong aromatic is made into a liqueur called Pimento Dram.

ANGELICA: (Garden Angelica, Holy Ghost; Latin: Angelica archangelica) A biennial plant that can attain a height of up to 2 metres before it blossoms, angelica has been cultivated throughout Europe since the 10th century, but grows wild in northern Scandinavian countries. Used to strengthen the immune system and to ward off certain fungal and bacterial infections, it was believed that an angel revealed angelica's ability to cure the plague. Others claim the plant was thusly named because it blooms on the feast of Saint Michael the Archangel (8 May). The dried roots and seeds have an aroma that is similar to juniper. Its character begins lightly sweet and warms to a bitter finish with a hint of musk. These qualities explain why angelica appears in the recipes for many gins, vermouths, Chartreuse, Bénédictine, Dubonnet, Campari, and aromatic bitters. And according to Margaret Grieve's 1931 *A Modern Herbal* "the Muscatel grape-like flavour of some wines, made on both sides of the Rhine, is (or is suspected to be) due to the secret use of angelica."

ANISE: (Latin: Pimpinella anisum) Anise in both wild and cultivated forms has been cherished for its culinary and medicinal uses in cultures around the world. The dried fruit—or so-called seeds—are very aromatic with a distinctive sweet and spicy character. Anise flowers are used to make Liquore Alchermes. Distilled from the fruits of both anise and star anise, oil of anise is a key element in the production of anisette, whilst the seeds are employed in vermouth and absinthe production.

Illicium anisatum L.

ANISE, STAR: (Chinese Anise; Latin: Illicum verum) Chewed to promote digestion and sweeten the breath, star anise is the more intensely aromatic Oriental relative of Anise. A mainstay in many Asian cuisines, Star Anise's strong licorice aroma and sweet character are most notable in Galliano liqueur, Sambuca, many pastis and absinthe recipes as well as vermouths and amaros.

ARTICHOKE: (See Cardoon.)

BALM: (See Lemon Balm.)

BAY LAUREL: (Laurel, Sweet Bay; Latin: Laurus nobilis) The backbone of many European and Indian cuisines, bay leaf is a pungent botanical that bears a similar aroma to oregano and thyme. It was administered as a tea to induce an appetite. This small tree has been cultivated in the Near East since recorded history and spread throughout the Mediterranean. A shrub version was even cultivated, beginning in the 1500s, in Britain because of its immense popularity as a culinary ingredient. In addition to being in some vermouths, bay laurel also appears in the recipes for a few herbal liqueurs and the bay laurel's berries are the main ingredient in Liqueur de Laurier.

BLESSED THISTLE: (Holy Thistle, Cnicus; Latin: Cnicus benedictus) A southern European native, this tall, slender flower bears leaves that when dried were commonly steeped as a tea to induce perspiration and as a remedy for intestinal worms. In addition to its use in some vermouths, blessed thistle was a popular ingredient in a few 19th-century aromatic bitters formulas.

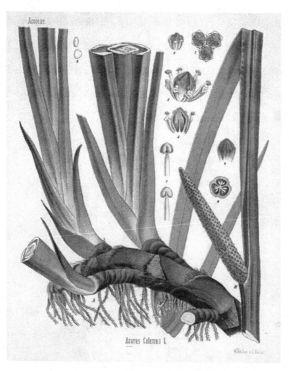

CALAMUS: (Sweet Sedge, Sweet Flag; Latin: Acorus calamus) An aquatic, reed-like plant that grows along lakes and streams as well as in marshes, calamus grows everywhere in Europe—except for Spain—plus Russia, Siberia, China, Japan, parts of eastern Europe, the Middle East, Sri Lanka, and India. Because of its distinctive sweet aroma, fresh Calamus was strewn on church floors during religious festivals and sometimes replaced the use of rushes in households. The root was often paired with angelica in 17th-century British soup and sauce recipes. Calamus root was also a popular botanical in 19th-century aromatic bitters such as Stockton

Bitters as well as American wine bitters because its bitter character served as an excellent substitute for the blend of cinnamon, nutmeg, and ginger. A key element in Campari and some gin recipes, calamus also features in the formulas for a few ales and vermouths.

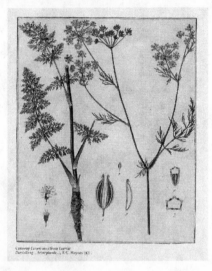

Caraway *Carum carvi* from Garcke *Darstellung ... Arzneipande...*, F.G. Haynes 1831.

CARAWAY: (Latin: Carum carvi) Growing in the northern and central regions of Europe and Asia, caraway is a biennial plant just like angelica, but only grows to about a half a metre in height. According to some historical literature, the ancient Arabs were the first to refer to caraway fruits as "seeds", prized for their distinctive aroma and character. Frequently appearing in recipes ranging from breads, cheeses, soups, cakes, and desserts, caraway is also an ingredient in liqueurs such as L'Huile de Venus, the feature flavour in Kümmel, and appears in some vermouth recipes.

CARDAMOM: (Elachi; Latin: Elettaria Cardamomum) The dried, ripe seeds of this southern India native are the third most expensive spice one can buy after saffron and vanilla. Cardamom is a familiar element in curry powder and masala chai and in a few Scandinavian and American pastry recipes. Well known for its use as an aid to digestion, this intensely aromatic spice with its sweet, warm character is frequently paired with orange, cinnamon, clove, or caraway. Cardamom schnapps, cardamom liqueur, Liquore Strega, Liquore Alchermes, as well as a few gins, pastis, and vermouths employ this spicy, yet citrusy botanical.

CALISAYA: (See Cinchona.)

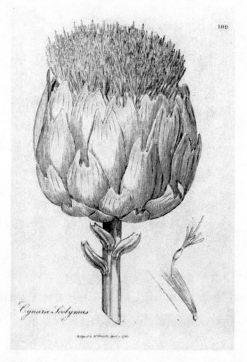

CARDOON: (Artichoke; Latin: Cynara cardunculus) A member of the thistle family, cardoons have been prized over the centuries for the green flowers—the artichokes—they produce. Disocorides and Pliny extolled its virtues. Besides its use as a food source, cardoons also produce a good yellow dye. The down at the artichoke's centre is steeped to make a rennet substitute used in Spain for the production of various cheeses. Cynar, a popular Italian bitter apéritif, is made from artichoke and a host other herbs. With its bittersweet character, artichoke is also regarded as a digestive. Hence, it is included in some vermouth recipes.

Croton Eluteria Bennet

CASCARILLA: (Eleutheria, Aromatic Quinquina; Latin: Croton eluteria) The bark of the dimunuative Bahamian native, the cascarilla tree, is known for its warm and bitter character. It was sometimes mixed with tobacco, lending to the smoking blend a slightly musky aroma. Cascarilla leaves were steeped as a digestive tea. And the bark is commonly paired with cinchona in aromatic bitters and in vermouths.

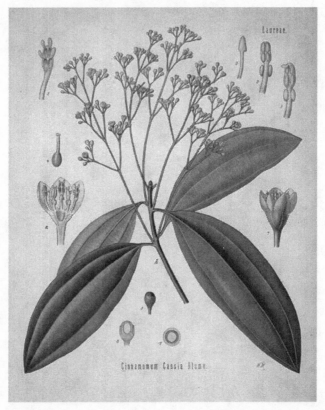

Cinnamomum Cassia Blume.

CASSIA: (Chinese Cinnamon, Bastard Cinnamon; Latin: Cinnamomum aromaticum) Frequently employed as a substitute for cinnamon, cassia is sometimes called "bastard cinnamon". Native to China, cassia trees are also cultivated throughout southeast Asia and Sri Lanka as well as Mexico and South America. The dried bark has the same aroma and character as cinnamon. This sweet, spicy alternative sometimes appears in place of or in addition to cinnamon in both gin and vermouth recipes.

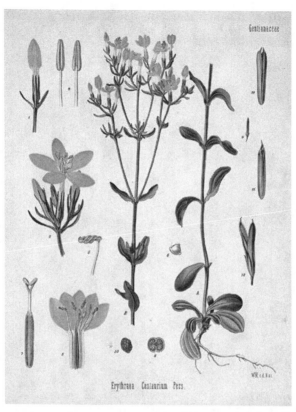

Erythraea Centaurium Pers.

CENTAURY: (Centaury Gentian, Red Centuary; Latin: Centarium erythraea) The dry pastures and chalky cliffs of Europe and north Africa are the home of this annual, which ancient Greeks called the "Gall of the Earth" because of its extreme bitterness. Known in Britain as felwort, this plant was gathered and dried for use as a treatment for heartburn, poor appetite, and dyspepsia. Centuary was one of the major herbs mixed with germander and yellow bugle in Portland Powder, an extremely popular gout medication. Centaury appears in aromatic bitters, herbal liqueurs such as Weltenburg Kloster, and vermouths.

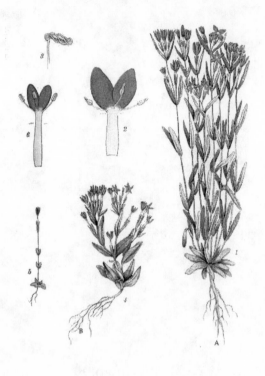

A. ARUN, CENTAURIUM VULGARE RAFN.
B. DVÄRGARUN, CENTAURIUM PULCHELLUM (SW.) DRUCE.

CENTAURY, LESSER: (Branched Centuary, Petite Centaury; Latin: Centaurium pulchellum) Another member of the gentian family, lesser centuary is a European native found near sand dunes and estuaries. It bears a similar profile to its cousin centuary and for the same reason is included in some vermouth recipes.

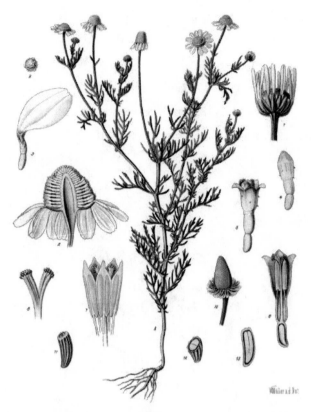

CHAMOMILE, COMMON: (Manzanilla, Maythen; Latin: Matricaria recutita) The most beloved of garden herbs, chamomile is a ground-cover plant with familiar, daisy-like blooms. Its distinct apple aroma and dry character not only delighted the ancient Greeks, it belies its mild bitterness. Known for its soothing affect on the nervous system, chamomile tea was sometimes combined with ginger to relive digestive ailments and systems of gout. Infused in spirit, chamomile was prescribed as a general tonic. Over 50% of the chamomile grown in France is devoted to Noilly Prat's vermouth production alone. But this herb is also a featured element in Marolo (an Italian grappa-based liqueur), in Manzanilla sherries, in chamomile wine, in Licor de Manzanilla (a Menorcan liqueur), some absinthe recipes, and in Liqueur de Camomile (a French liqueur).

CHERVIL, SWEET: (Sweet Cicely, British Myrrh; Latin: Anthriscus cerefolium) A northern British and Scot native, this very aromatic perennial also abounds along mountain pastures from the Pyrenees to the Caucausus. With a celery-like aroma that is similar to Lovage and an anise-like character, sweet chervil was commonly prescribed as an appetite stimulant and appears in some German food recipes.

This plant is not the same as the southern European native, chervil, which is part of the French culinary blend—*fines herbes*—and possesses faint liquorice notes.

CICELY, SWEET: (See Chervil, Sweet.)

Cinchona succirubra Pav

CINCHONA: (Calisaya, Quinine Bark; Latin: Cinchona officinalis) There is more than one species of cinchona tree that displays fragrant white and pink blooms in the tropical valleys of South America. The two varieties that were most valued by pharmacists, herbalists, and distillers are Cinchona succirubra and Cinchona calisaya. Named after the Countess of Chinchon, who first introduced the bark in Europe for its medicinal qualities, cinchona yields a high level of quinine. (Because of quinine's anti-malarial virtues, cinchona is also cultivated in Java, India, and Sri Lanka.) An intensely astringent and bitter botanical, cinchona imparts only the faintest aroma. Besides being the key ingredient in Liqueur di China Calisaia, Ferro China, Aperol, China-Martini, and Liquore Calisaya, it is also present in many aromatic bitters, digestive bitters, and vermouths.

CINNAMON: (Latin: Cinnamomum verum) Not to be confused with cassia, a spice that is frequently sold as cinnamon in the United States, true cinnamon from the Cinnamomum zeylanicum tree is native to Sri Lanka. Due to its popularity, it has been cultivated in Indonesia, Sumatra, India, Brazil, and other areas. The Dutch East India Company owned the monopoly on wild cinnamon until the late 1770s, when it was finally cultivated to meet the demand.

The dried bark emits a fragrant aroma and a distinctive sweet, warm, spicy character that is widely used in cooking and as a treatment for digestive ailments. Besides its use in gin and vermouth formulas, cinnamon is the featured ingredient in cinnamon schnapps and liqueur. (See also Cassia.)

CLARY: (See Sage, Clary.)

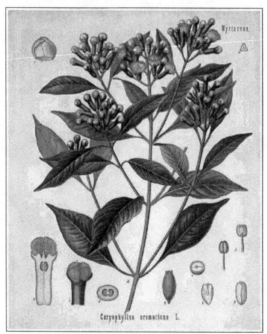

CLOVE: (Latin: Syzygium aromaticum) Indonesia's Malaku Islands are the origin of this highly aromatic spice tree, which yields clusters of long, undeveloped flowers that are dried to become cloves. Cultivated in both the East and West Indies as well as Madagascar, Tanzania, Sri Lanka, and Brazil, clove entered the European culinary and medical repertoires during the fourth century. It has historically been chewed to relieve toothache pain as it is a mild topical anaesthetic. Despite its woody stems, cloves are delicate and quickly lose potency if not properly stored. Clove is one of the botanicals featured in Bénédictine, clove schnapps, Liqueur Tentura, aromatic bitters, and vermouths.

CORIANDER: (Latin: Coriandrum sativum) A striking annual that spread from its southern European birthplace to Britain when it was imported by the Romans, wild and cultivated coriander leaves and seeds appear in numerous dishes because of their mildly aromatic flavour. Regarded as an excellent appetite stimulant, coriander is frequently paired with angelica, gentian, quassia, and lavender in aromatic bitters. Besides its employment in vermouths, pastis, and gins, coriander is also an ingredient in Galliano Liqueur and Eau de Canes.

CNICUS: (See Blessed Thistle.)

CROCUS: (See Saffron.)

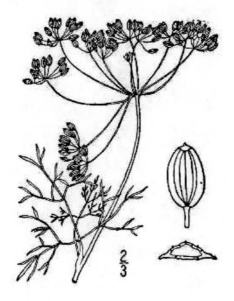

DILL: (Latin: Anethum graveolens) An annual well known throughout the Mediterranean and southern Russia, dill resembles fennel in its structure and was highly regarded by ancient Greeks and Romans for its culinary and medicinal virtues. Its seeds are pungent and lightly bitter. The entire plant is aromatic, although the volatile oils in the leaves are very fragile and are regarded as a slightly sweet herb. Employed as an appetite stimulant, dill is infused into a schnapps and is included in some vermouth recipes.

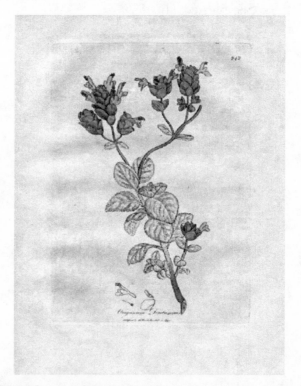

DITTANY OF CRETE: (Hop Majoram; Latin: Origanum Dictamus) Famed for being the plant steeped with wormwood in wine by Hippocrates, the dittany of Crete grows wild along Crete's mountainsides and gorges. Prized as a token of love, many people lost their lives while gathering dittany flowers in this craggy and treacherous landscape. Hippocrates found this herb to be helpful in treating digestive complaints. The plant has become so rare that it is now protected by European Union law. Yet it is a key ingredient used in some vermouth and absinthe formulas as well as in perfume recipes, and it is still harvested by locals and used as an herbal tea.

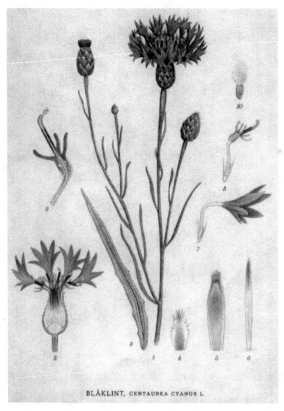

BLÅKLINT, CENTAUREA CYANUS L.

EGYPTIAN CORNFLOWER: (Latin: Centaurea cyanus) Providing striking colour, it is no wonder that cornflower juice was used to make blue ink and a temporary dye. Dried, the petals were added to potpourris simply for their colour. Similar to blessed thistle, it was infused as a tea to induce perspiration and as an appetite stimulant. In addition to its use in the production of some vermouths, Egyptian corn-flower was an ingredient found in some 19th-century aromatic bitters formulas.

ENEBRO: (See Juniper.)

ELACHI: (See Cardamom.)

ELDER: (Eldrum, Bore Tree; Latin: Sambucus nigra) A familiar sight throughout the British countryside, the elder tree's fragrant, white flowers herald the beginning of summer. Its blackish-purple berries signal its finale. Although the bark, the leaves, and berries have a myriad of practical uses in the home and the pharmacy, the delicate blossoms are the most prized harvest. The floral clusters are infused with vinegar for dressing salads and to relieve a sore throat. They are fermented with yeast to make a sparkling wine and distilled to make elderflower water. Besides a distinctive Muscat-wine aroma, elderflowers have a dry, crisp character that lends itself for use in elderflower liqueur and schnapps as well as vermouth recipes.

ELECAMPANE: (Elf Dock, Horseheal; Latin: Inula hele-nium) Growing wild throughout Europe, southern Siberia, and northwest India, elecampane can be found in damp pastures and shady areas. A statuesque plant with large, bright yellow flowers, this perennial was cultivated for its culinary and medicinal uses. Like angelica stems, elecampane roots were candied and consumed as a confection. Amongst its many uses, the herb was employed to improve the digestion as well as for its pungent, bitter astringency. A prime ingredient in the production of Swiss and French absinthe, elecampane is also included in some vermouth recipes. A liqueur was also made by infusing the roots along with currants in white port. It is also the feature ingredient in an herbal wine called Vin d'Aulnée.

FENNEL, FLORENCE: (Finocchio; Latin: Foeniculum vulgare) Another perennial that grows wild throughout temperate Europe, especially in areas with limestone soils or chalk cliffs, fennel is cultivated in France, Russia, India, and Persia. Ancient Romans favoured its edible shoots and aromatic fruits. Aromatic fennel seeds possess a warm, sweet character and were administered as a tea to relive gastric distress. Florence fennel (aka: finocchio) is one of the three main ingredients used in absinthe production. Some liqueurs and akavits are flavoured with fennel. It is also used in some vermouths and pastis.

FLAG, SWEET: (See Calamus.)

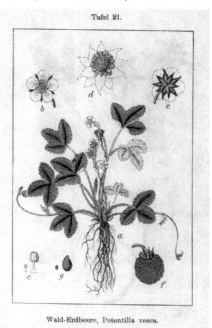

Tafel 21.

Wald-Erdbeere, Potentilla vesca.

FRAISES DES BOIS: (Wild Strawberry, Alpine Strawberry; Latin: Fragaria vasca) This delicate cousin of the cultivated strawberry produces the berries that provide the distinctive aroma and character of Chambéryzette, a unique vermouth that is flavoured with fraises des bois juice. The berries are also a key ingredient in Fragoli and fraises des bois liqueurs. In medicine, the berries of this everbearing woodland plant were administered to relieve gout. Ancient Persians were the first to cultivate these diminuative berries.

GALANGAL: (China Root, Galanga; Latin: Kaempferia galanga) The dried rhizome of this southern Chinese native resembles ginger root and was employed to relieve sea sickness, gastric distress, and appetite loss. Aromatic galangal possesses a citrus, pine, and earth aroma with a pungent cedar and soap character. It is an essential ingredient in Thai and Vietnamese cuisine and is paired with gentian in Zoladkowa Gorzka, a flavoured Polish vodka. Some aromatic bitters, vermouth, beers, and even ginger ale recipes employ galangal.

GENEPY: (Spiked Wormwood; Latin: Artemesia genepi) An alpine cousin of Artemesia absinthium, genepy variety proliferates throughout the Pyrenees and the Alps. The Carthusian monks responsible for producing Chartreuse also formulated a Génépi des Pêres Chartreux liqueur that features this somewhat vegetal charactered bitter herb which resembles chamomile. There are a number of génépi liqueur producers who also make Fleurs des Alpes and Fio d'Alpi liqueurs which include genepy. A Basque liqueur known as Izarra infuses the flowers into both its green and yellow versions. White genepy (Artemesia glacialis) is a rarer species that is included in some absinthe and vermouth recipes as well as aromatic bitters.

GENTIAN: (Spring Gentian, Latin: Gentiana verna; Yellow Gentian, Latin: Gentiana lutea) There are more than 180 species of this alpine flower that grow in the world's temperate and high mountain regions, including the century family. Two varieties of gentain in particular have starring roles in brewing and distillation—yellow gentian and spring gentian. Yellow gentian grows in the mountains and lower slopes of central and southern Europe. Known for its intensely bitter properties and slight sweet foretaste, the roots are the primary ingredient in Suze and an essential element in Aperol, Campari, Zoladkowa Gorzka, Angostura bitters, Moxie, Genziana beer, Bundaberg Brewing Company's Bitters Brew, some vermouths, and Tyrolian Gentian Schnapps, which also uses the blossoms of the spring gentian.

GENTIAN, CENTUARY: (See Centaury.)

GERMANDER, COMMON: (Wall Germander, Petit Chêne; Latin: Teucrium chamaedrys) With an aroma that resembles garlic and a bitter, pungent character, germander leaves were specifically prescribed to relieve gout (germander leaves are a key ingredient in Portland Powder) and its flowers were infused in wine to dispel intestinal worms. A European and Near East native, this creeping evergeen provided one of the prime ingredients in an ancient Greek formula called theriac, a powerful antidote. Appearing in vermouth, herbal liqueurs, and aromatic bitters recipes, germander was also used to stimulate a poor appetite and relieve anorexia.

GINGER: (Latin: Zingiber officinale) The quintessential Asian culinary spice, ginger root is closely related to galangal and cardamom in the plant world. Cultivated not only in Asia but in East Africa and the Caribbean, ginger's pungent yet sweet aroma and character is valued in both sweet and savoury dishes. Effective in the treatment of sea sickness, ginger-based drinks including ginger ale and ginger beer are often recommended to settle an upset stomach. In addition to ginger liqueurs, this ingredient also appears in aromatic bitters and vermouths.

HINDBERRY: (See Raspberry.)

HOPS: (Latin: Humulus Lupulus) A British native that grows wild in hedges and copses, the twining hops yields female flowers used extensively by the brewing industry, appearing in Dutch recipes as early as the 1300s and in British recipes since the 1500s. A bitter herb with a very familiar aroma, Hops was combined with marjoram, wormwood, yarrow, or germander and broom in ale recipes. Infused in sherry, hops were given as a stomach cordial to improve the appetite and soothe indigestion. An aromatic bitters that included angelica and blessed thistle was a common folk preparation. Not surprisingly, hops appears in some vermouth recipes.

HORSEHEAL: (See Elecampane.)

HYSSOP: (Latin: Hyssopus officinalis) Used for cleansing sacred sites back in Dioscorides' day, hyssop is a lovely evergeen bush that yields royal blue blossoms. The entire plant has culinary and medicinal value. But its strong, bitter, minty aroma and character are an important to the production of Chartreuse, a few herbal liqueurs, and vermouths.

IRIS, FLORENTINE: (See Orris root.)

JAMAICA PEPPER: (See Allspice.)

JUNIPER, COMMON: (Enebro; Latin: Juniperus communis) The small common juniper evergreen can be found throughout Europe, North Africa and northern Asia. Technically, it does not produce berries, but small pine cones with unusually fleshy and merged scales generally referred to as berries. The berry's light piney aroma and sweet pine taste are found in gin, genever, and genièvre. In Sweden, there is a beer that is flavoured with common juniper berrries. Well known for its merits as a treatment for indigestion and gastric ailments, a juniper liqueur called Junivere was a popular

Dutch health elixir. Given its widespread popularity for its piney character, it is no surprise that it also appears in a few vermouth recipes.

LAUREL: (See Bay Laurel.)

LAVENDER, FRENCH: (Latin: Lavandula Stoechas) A variety of the lavender shrub that was favoured for its aroma by the ancient Romans and Libyans, French lavender grows not only in France, but throughout Spain and Portugal. Unlike English lavender, this variety has an aroma that resembles rosemary and was one of the ingredients in Four Thieves Vinegar or Four Thieves Wine along with clary sage, thyme, rosemary, garlic, and sometimes wormwood. Lavender conserves were prepared as a condiment and the flowers used to flavour dishes "to comfort the stomach." Its flowers are a common element in perfumes. The dried tops are included in some vermouth, liqueur, and aromatic bitters recipes.

LEMON BALM: (Balm, Sweet Balm; Latin: Melissa officinalis) This southern European native grows in mountainous regions and was naturalized in southern England, where it is appreciated for its fragrant, citrusy aroma and its delicate, cooling character. An ingredient in Claret Cup, lemon balm also appears in liqueur, schnapps and vermouth recipes. it is an essential ingredient in Absente, an absinthe substitute, and in some absinthes.

LIQUORICE: (Licorice; Latin: Glycyrrhiza glabra) Liquorice shrubs may be native to southeastern Europe and southwestern Asia, but they are cultivated in in other countries including Russia and Britain. The roots are not dissimilar in character and medical use to anise, fennel, and star anise, which is why this sweet herb appears in pastis, absinthe, and some vermouth recipes as well as in numerous liqueurs and schnapps.

LUNGÖRT, PULMONARIA OFFICINALIS L.

LUNGWORT: (Pulmonaria, Bethlehem Sage, Soldiers and Sailors; Latin: Pulmonaria officinalis) An evergreen perennial that is a close cousin to Borage, lungwort is favoured by gardeners for its white-spotted green leaves and delicate violet coloured flowers. This herb is frequently confused with lung moss or lungwort lichen, which is the actual ingredient used in brewing. The leaves of this plant are sometimes used in vermouth recipes.

LUNGWORT: (Lung Moss, Lungwort Lichen, Tree Lungwort; Latin: Sticta pulmonaria) Growing along coastal areas in Europe, Asia, Africa, and North America, this lichen is an endangered species that was a popular folk and traditional remedy for bronchial conditions just like its floral namesake. But the leaves of this plant were also used for making orange dye, tanning leather, as a fixative in perfumes, and as an ingredient in brewing as well vermouth recipes.

MACE: (Muscadier; Latin: Myristica fragans) A small evergreen tree that grows in the Moluccas, West Indies, India, Java, and Sumatra, the fruits of the nutmeg tree are also the source of mace. The fleshy inner skin surrounding the "nut" of this fruit is what is dried and called mace. With properties identical to those of nutmeg, mace was provided as a digestive aid to patients weak stomachs. In European cuisine, mace appears in savoury dishes as well as in pastries. Appearing side by side with Nutmeg, Mace's warm, sweet aroma and taste explains why it appears in recipes for Créme d'Absynth, a few Alpine apéritifs and vermouth. This spice should not be confused with English mace, which is a flowering, aromatic perennial discovered, in 1798, in Switzerland and cultivated throughout northern Europe.

MARJORAM, WILD: (Oregano; Latin: Origanum vulgare) A perennial herb that frequently appears in the culinary and medical repertoire, wild marjoram was recognized by ancient

Greeks and Romans for its balsamic and light camphor aroma as well as its warm, bitter character. One of the many uses found for the dried leaves was a warm infusion that was administered to relieve dyspepsia and stomach ailments. A specialty in Avignon, Les Paplines d'Avignon liqueur combines chocolate and wild marjoram. Thriving throughout Europe, Asia, and North Africa, wild marjoram also figures into vermouth and angelica liqueur.

MILFOIL, MUSK: (See Musk Yarrow.)

MYRRH, BRITISH: (See Chervil.)

NUTMEG: (Latin: Myristica fragrans) The same, small evergreen tree that is the source of mace, also yields nutmeg—the kernel of the nutmeg's fruit. Grown in the Moluccas, West Indies, India, Java, and Sumatra, the fruit kernels were found to be an excellent digestive aid for stomach weakness and a gastro-intestinal stimulant. Just like mace, nutmeg occasionally appears in absinthe and vermouth recipes. (see also Mace)

OREGANO: (See Majoram, Wild.)

Iris florentina L.

ORRIS ROOT: (Florentine Iris; Latin: Iris Florentina) A symbol of power and majesty in Roman and Egyptian times, ornamental Florentine irises are native to the eastern Mediterranean, but have spread into North Africa and the Near East. They are cultivated on mountain slopes throughout southern Europe. The rhizomes of this beautiful perennial possess a violet-like aroma and bitter-sweet character that is used in perfumes (not only as a scent, but also as a fixer) and as well as in gin, curaçao, absinthe, some amaros, aromatic bitters, and vermouth because it has the power to enhance other botanical aromas.

PULMONARIA: (See Lungwort.)

QUASSIA: (Bitter Wood, Surinan Quassia; Latin; Quassia amara) A towering inhabitant of Brazil, the heartwood of the Quassia amara tree has an intensely bitter taste but relatively little aroma. Taken as a tea with ginger, quassia was found useful for treating anorexia and impaired digestion. Its is used to impart bitter flavours in apéritifs, vermouth, and aromatic bitters.

QUININE BARK: (See Cinchona.)

QUINQUINA: (See Cascarilla.)

RASPBERRY: (Hindberry; Latin: Rubus idaeus) Growing wild in part of Britain, the Raspberry is a European native. A shrubby biennial with creeping perennial roots, it is cultivated and cherished for its fragrant fruit. Used for making fruit-based wine, vinegar, and brandy, the fruit is also used to make a dye. However, Raspberry leaves are also useful.

Served as a tea to relieve stomach complaints, they have astringent and mildly bitter properties. Raspberry fruits are the basis for making Chambord, Framboise liqueur, a Belgiam lambic beer, and a few vermouths.

RHUBARB, ENGLISH: (Garden Rhubarb; Latin: Rheum rhabarbarum) Of the three different types of rhubarb grown, English rhubarb is best known for its nutritive and medicinal value in the relief of stomach troubles. Mildly astringent and distinctly citric in flavour, rhubarb stems are used in liqueurs, in amaros such as Zucca, in vermouths, and in aromatic bitters.

ROSIER DE PROVINS.

ROSE, PROVINS: (Latin: Rosa gallica officinalis) The basis for the liqueurs L'Huile de Rose and Parfait Amour as well as Rosolio, Spirit of Roses, and some vermouths, fragrant Provins Roses (aka: Rosa gallica) are distilled into rose water, made into rose conserve and syrup, and used in confections, savoured for their astringent character and delicate aroma. The ancient Romans were reputedly the first to recognize this rose variety's virtues and cultivate it, garnishing their Falernian wine with its petals.

Rosmarinus officinalis L.

ROSEMARY: (Polar Plant, Compass Plant; Latin: Rosmarinus officinalis) This evergreen shrub has been well-known since ancient times for its earthy, piny aroma and buttery, piny taste. Burnt along with juniper berries to purify the air and prevent infection, rosemary was used for its fragrance—a practice that continued well into the Second World War in French hospitals. Rosemary is an essential ingredient in the manufacture of eau-de-cologne and a key culinary ingredient in more than a few European cultures. Made into an herbal wine, a tea, and a conserve, rosemary was believed to tone the stomach and stimulate the appetite. It is incorporated into numerous herbal liqueurs, vermouths, amaros, and aromatic bitters.

Ruta graveolens L.

RUE: (Herby Grass, Herb of Grace; Latin: Ruta graveolens) A hardy, intensely fragrant southern European evergreen, rue was introduced to Britain by the ancient Romans who encouraged its cultivation. Ancient Greeks regarded it as a remedy for nervous indigestion caused by eating with strangers. As bitter as it is fragrant, rue is sometimes added to grappa to make grappa alla ruta. Difficult to harvest because the leaves and volatile oils can cause blistering when the skin is exposed to sunlight just like hogweed, rue is sparingly used in some vermouth and amaro recipes.

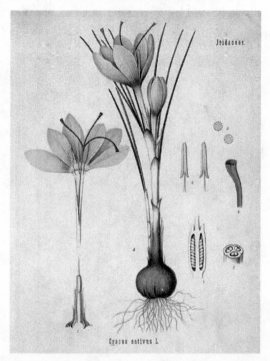

Crocus sativus L.

SAFFRON: (Crocus; Latin Crocus sativus) One of the world's most expensive spices, Saffron is an ornamental plant with large, lily-shaped flowers that was well known to ancient Hebrews, Assyrians, Greeks, and Romans. The flower's stigmas are of great value because it takes about

60,000 of them to yield 500 grams of saffron. The yellow dye derived from these tender threads is prized in Asia and its aroma is likened to perfume—a blend of metallic honey with fresh hay notes. (Tumeric is commonly known as the "poor man's saffron" because it has many similar qualities.) Used in confections and savoury dishes, saffron is also used to make an herbal liqueur called Paan, Strega, Licor de Oro, some vermouths, and a few amaros.

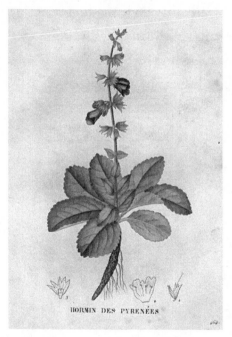

HORMIN DES PYRENÉES

SAGE, CLARY: (Common Clary, Clammy Sage; Latin: Salvia sclarea) A native of Syria, Italy, southern France, and Switzerland, clary sage has been cultivated in Britain since the late 1500s, where this biennial plant was used by brewers as an alternative to hops. A country wine fermented with this flowering herb tastes similar to Frontignac wine. A tea made from this herb was used as an appetite stimulant. Believed to be a protectant against bubonic plague, clary sage was steeped with lavender, thyme, rosemary, garlic, and sometimes wormwood to create Four Thieves Wine or Four Thieves Vinegar. The perfume industry relies on its distinctive aroma and similarity to ambergris as a fixer in perfume formulation. Herbalists made alcoholic tinctures, combining clary sage, chamomile, caraway, and coriander seed to treat digestive disorders. Liqueur à La Sauge is sometimes made with clary sage instead of common sage.

SAGE, COMMON: (Garden Sage; Latin: Saliva officinalis) Cultivated for many culinary and medicinal purposes down the centuries, Sage grows wild along the European Mediterranean. Containing a higher level of the active chemical thujone, sage shares the same bitter character as wormwood and oregano. Liqueur à La Sauge relies on sage's aroma and character as do some vermouths and amaros.

Santalum album

SANDALWOOD, RED: (Sanders-wood; Latin: Santalum album) The small red sandalwood tree grown in southern India yields a wood that was highly valued during China's Ming and Qing dynasties. Its fragrant, woody aroma is an excellent fixative in perfume development and in some vermouth recipes.

SAVORY: (Summer Savory; Latin: Satureja hortensis; Winter Savory; Satureja montana) Savory is another standard garden herb that has made its way from its native habitat along the Mediterranean to being cultivated in Britain and the United States. Used in the same culinary manner as sage, summer savory is a favoured herb in Eastern European sausage and savoury dishes, imparting a strong, pungent character. Regarded as a digestive aid, the annual summer savory is less bitter than its relative, the perennial winter savory. While summer savory is used in some vermouth recipes, it is the winter savory that is favoured in herbal liqueur and amaro recipes.

SEDGE, SWEET: (See Calamus.)

SPEEDWELL: (Veronica; Latin: Veronica officinalis) The leaves of this perennial—which inhabits heaths, moors, and dry hedgebanks—was highly regarded by herbalists for its astringent and bitter, slightly tangy flavour. For this reason alone, speedwell is included in some vermouth and amaro recipes.

STRAWBERRY, ALPINE: (See Fraises des Bois)

STRAWBERRY, WILD: (See Fraises des Bois)

TEAZLE, COMMON: (Teasel, Teazel, Card Thistle, Church Broom; Latin: Disacus fullonum) Found in hedgerows and wastelands throughout Europe and Asia, the prickly teazle yields roots with a bitter, warm, and pungent flavour that were infused into a tea and administered to strengthen the stomach and stimulate the appetite. Liquori Casalinghi 89, Pelinkovac, plus some aromatic bitters, amaros, and vermouths include teazle.

THYME, COMMON: (Garden Thyme; Latin: Thymus vulgaris) A hardy perennial, thyme has long been regarded as a faithful companion to lavender. The dried leaves are infused as a tea to arrest gastric fermentation. Used in savory dishes, thyme yields a fragrant aroma that is familiarly blended into *bouquet garni* and *herbes de Provence*. Farigoule is a liqueur whose base element is thyme. There are also a few amaros and vermouths that include thyme in their recipes.

TONKA BEAN: (Tonquin Bean; Latin: Dipteryx odorata) A forest tree native to Brazil and British Guiana, the tonka yields beans that are sometimes used as a vanilla substitute. With an aroma similar to a blend of vanilla, almonds, cinnamon, and clove, tonka is used in the perfume industry as well in the manufacture of some aromatic bitters, amaros, and vermouths.

TUMERIC: (Latin: Curcuma longa) A perennial plant from the ginger family with a rhizome that looks like orange-coloured ginger root, tumeric is a tropical south Asian native and yields a deep orange-yellow powder when dried. Used as a spice in Asian and Middle Eastern cuisine, tumeric imparts its colour and dry taste to many dishes—a cheaper alternative to saffron. It is for this same reason its is used as a cheap dye for textiles and cosmetics. Its mustardy aroma and distinctly earthy, slightly bitter, slightly hot pepper character are reasons why its appears in some vermouths as a saffron substitute.

VANILLA BEAN: (Latin: Vanilla planifolia) Vanilla orchids, found in Central America with various subspecies grown in Madagascar and other tropical islands in the Indian Ocean, yield the world's second most expensive spice next to saffron—vanilla beans. The fruits when dried yield a strongly sweet aromatic aroma and character with obvious culinary uses. It is also a prized element in the perfume industry and is a key ingredient in Galliano liqueur and a few amaros.

VERONICA: (See Speedwell.)

VERVEINE, FRENCH: (Lemon Verbena; Latin: Lippia citriodora) Also known as lemon verbena and verveine odorante, French verveine is a fragrant native of Argentina, Chile and Peru. Spanish explorers imported this low-growing shrub to Europe, in the 1600s, where its was named Aloysia triphylla after the princess Maria Louisa of Parma. Herbalists believed that French verveine's soothing yet refreshingly lemony aroma provided a calming effect on the nervous system, aided digestion and relieved mild depression. Its dry, soft citrus character, similar to lemongrass, compliments many bitter botanicals in vermouths, amaros, and herbal liqueurs.

VIOLET, SWEET: (Latin: Viola odorata) There are over 200 species of violet that grow on nearly every continent. But it is sweet violet that ancient Romans harvested to make an herbal wine. This variety figures in French and some British cuisine because of its floral aroma, which is very similar to orris root. Crème de Violette as well as a few herbal liqueurs, amaros, and vermouths take advantage of this sweet, floral quality.

Artemisia Absinthium L.

WORMWOOD, COMMON: (Green Ginger; Latin: Artemesia absinthium) An intensely bitter botanical that was
used to cure poor digestion and numerous other ailments,
common wormwood is one of the three types of wormwood
that ancient Greeks and Romans used to make a variety of
wormwood wines. A powerful appetite stimulant and digestive, there are few cultures that did not develop recipes and
a taste for wormwood wines, especially where the plant is a

native including Europe and Siberia. Common wormwood is an essential ingredient in nearly all vermouths, absinthes (where it is also imparts the spirit's distinctive green hue), and some aromatic bitters. Traditionally, wormwood flowers were also infused in brandy to relieve gout.

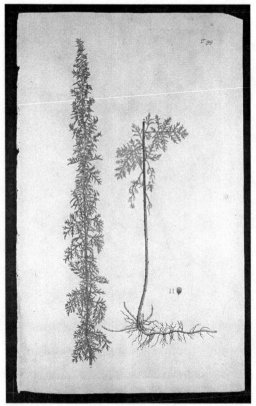

WORMWOOD, ROMAN: (Latin: Artemisia pontica) Far less bitter than common wormwood, this perennial shrub was once planted around the bases of grapevines. The root contact was enough to impart a bitter flavour to the resulting wine. Today, its lacy silvery green stalks make it popular with gardeners as a vigorous border plant. It is used in some absinthes, primarily to add its green colouring.

WORMWOOD, SPIKED: (See Genepy)

YARROW, MUSK: (Musk Milfoil; Latin: Achillea moschata) This alpine member of the yarrow family grows along the roadsides throughout Switzerland and surrounding mountainous regions. Used by herbalists as a tea to induce perspiration and as an astringent, musk yarrow possesses a distinctive musk aroma as well as a wormwood-with-peppermint character. The Swiss in the Engandine district combine this plant with a few others to make Espirit d'Iva Liqueur. Musk yarrow and its cousin yarrow (Latin: Achillea millefolium) also feature in some aromatic bitters recipes.

THE RIGHT BLEND

It is well known that the exact botanical proportions employed in today's vermouths are closely-guarded industry secrets. However, prior to this age of intellectual property rights and industrial espionage, vermouth and apéritif recipes appeared in household cookbooks, giving every family an opportunity to refine or enhance a basic formula to taste.

Take for example this recipe for Vermouth Breslau, which provides keen insight into the style of sweet wormwood wine that Wallenstein requested to be produced prior to his homecoming to Bohemia. Many estates and farms throughout Europe were equipped with distillation devices which were used to make eaux-de-vie and other spirits from the harvest. Poor farmers relied on travelling distillers who transported their equipment from house to house.

VERMOUTH BRESLAU
750 gr Common Wormwood leaves
150 gr Common Wormwood flowers
150 gr Blessed Thistle
40 gr Cloves
3.6 kg Sugar

6 litres Water
11 litres 80° Alcohol

Macerate and then distill 9.5 litres of middle cut spirit. Make a syrup with the sugar and water. Add to bring back the spirit to 40° and tint the liquid green.

Unlike these old-school wormwood wine recipes, vermouth formulations achieved a high level of sophistication by the 1900s, when examples were published in books such as the 1900 encyclopedia of the liquor industry, *Le Distillerie dans le Monde Entier*, and Manuels-Roret's 1918 edition of *Nouveau Manuel Complet du Disillateur Liquoriste*.

A simple Vermouth di Torino formula started with 95 litres of Moscato (or sweet Picpoul) wine into which botanicals were macerated for 5 days in the following proportions:

VERMOUTH DI TORINO
130 gr Germander
110 gr Chinese cinnamon
16 gr Nutmeg
130 gr Blessed Thistle
125 gr Calamus
120 gr Elecampane
130 gr Petite Centaury
130 gr Common Wormwood
65 gr Gentian
60 gr Angelica root
7 gr Fresh orange slices
5 litres 85° Neutral spirit

After 5 days, blend the mixture with isinglass (a marine collagen sometimes used to clarify wine and beer), allow to rest for 8 days, then strain and bottle.

Another vermouth called Olivero's Crop began with 100 litres of Picardan white wine to which the following botanicals were steeped for 6 days:

OLIVERO'S CROP
125 gr Common Wormwood
125 gr Blessed Thistle
125 gr Elecampane roots
125 gr Petite Centaury
125 gr Germander
100 gr Chinese cinnamon
60 gr Angelica root
50 gr Nutmeg
50 gr Galangal
50 gr Cloves
500 gr Coriander seeds
250 gr Bitter orange peel
250 gr Ground orris root
200 gr Elder Flowers
150 gr Red Cinchona
150 gr Calamus
300 litres   Cassis

After 6 days, blend the mixture with isinglass (a marine collagen sometimes used to clarify wine and beer), allow to rest for two weeks. Then strain. To make a premium quality vermouth, add 2 litres of an infusion of roasted bitter almonds with 3 litres of good brandy.

But not every recipe calls for the botanicals to be steeped in wine. Some changed the balance in favour of spirit, adding the wine as the finishing touch:

3 litres Alcohol 94°
1 kg Sugar
6 gr Chinese Cinnamon
2 gr Nutmegs
1 gr Orange
5 gr Petite centaury
12 gr Common Wormwood
6 gr Gentian
5 gr Angelica root
5 gr Blessed Thistle
5 gr Calamus
5 gr Elecampane

Steep the botanicals in spirit for 8 to 10 days. Add 1 litre of water plus 1.5 liters sugar syrup and 5 litres of sweet white wine.

Then a more complex, extremely bitter-based formula prescribed the infusion into 25 litres of ordinary white wine of the following:

50 gr Common Wormwood, stripped
50 gr Roman Wormwood
60 gr Sweet orange peel
20 gr Laraha peel (a bitter citrus fruit that is native to Curaçao)
55 gr Peach kernels
50 gr Oregano
5 gr Cina (Artemisia cina / Sagebrush of Judea)
15 gr Petite Centaury

60 gr Red Cinchona
50 gr Orris Root
60 gr Speedwell
60 gr Pulmonaria
60 gr Blessed Thistle
60 gr Elder Flowers
15 gr Germander
8 gr Rhubarb

After infusion (of about 6 days), train and add 2 liters of 40° eau-de-vie and 1 kilo of burnt sugar to the wine.

A TOUCH OF ART PLUS SPIRIT

From this small representation of recipes, it's clear to see that not all vermouths followed or follow the wine plus plants followed by spirit production structure. Neither is it true that all vermouths use a wine eau-de-vie or brandy as the finishing touch, the fortification that preserves the sweetness of the wine and the strength of the botanical blend. Cognac, neutral grain spirit, even cassis (not the liqueur, but its namesake blackcurrant distillate) were viable alternatives.

What all aromatized wines do require is artistry. It takes the knowledge and expertise of a botanist to source supplies of these natural ingredients, which can vary in potency from growing season to growing season, and may or may not remain stable after harvest. The experience of a trained vintner is essential to identifying and properly fermenting grapes than can deliver the balance of sweetness and acidity in a finished wine—the counterfoil to the essential botancial bitterness and spiciness. Finally, the distiller's comprehension of alcohol's natural ability to retard fermentation, preserve the botanicals' aroma, character, and potency guarantees that the final result delivers the symphony of flavours expected from vermouth.

With personalities that are as individualistic as their makers, it's now time to survey today's family of vermouths and their close apéritif relations.

CHAPTER FOUR
VERMOUTH & APÉRITIFS TODAY

An estimated 20 million litres of vermouth are produced and consumed annually worldwide. Unlike so many drinks where consumption is fairly uniform, a cultural rift divides American and European (and European-influenced South American and South Pacific) vermouth drinkers. Americans in Europe have a long history of ordering a "Martini" and being shocked to receive a goblet of Martini Bianco vermouth on ice. To a lesser extent, French and Italian visitors to America have been surprised to discover a "Martini" has lots of gin and very little "Martini". More surprising to Europeans visiting the States is how many people there have never tasted straight vermouth. It has been so ingrained into American culture through jokes about dry martinis, and the public spontaneously taking those jokes and weaving them into the social fabric.

Fortunately, the veil of misunderstanding is lifting as the new cocktail renaissance reaches further and further into the heartlands of America and Europe. Both sides are gaining a greater understanding of and respect for vermouth and vermouth cocktails.

THE PRODUCERS & THEIR PRODUCTS

An estimated twenty million litres of vermouth are produced and consumed annually worldwide. Unlike so many drinks where consumption is fairly uniform, a cultural rift divides American and European (and European-influenced South American and South Pacific) vermouth drinkers. Americans in Europe have a long history of ordering a "Martini" and being shocked to receive a goblet of Martini Bianco vermouth on ice. To a lesser extent, French and Italian visitors to America have been surprised to discover a "Martini" has lots of gin and very little "Martini". More surprising to Europeans visiting the States is how many people there have never tasted straight vermouth. It has been so ingrained into American culture through jokes about dry martinis, and the public spontaneously taking those jokes and weaving them into the social fabric.

Fortunately, the veil of misunderstanding is lifting as the new cocktail renaissance reaches further and further into the heartlands of America and Europe. Both sides are gaining a greater understanding of and respect for vermouth and vermouth cocktails.

Amaro Lucano S.p.a., Pisticci, Italy

www.amarolucano.it

Developed by the Vena family who owned Bar Vena in Pisticci, in 1894, this amaro received a duchal warrant from the House of Savoy.

PRODUCT: Amaro Lucano

NOTES: Nine known botanicals such as gentian, angelica, rue, sage, thyme, and juniper are included along with other botanicals in a hot maceration. 30% ABV

Averna S.p.A., Caltanissetta, Italy

www.averna.it

Salvatore Averna was born in 1802 into a well-off family of textile merchants. He grew up in Caltanissetta, becoming a judge and benefactor of the Convent of St. Spirito's

Abbey in nearby Fruili. The Benedictine friars of that abbey produced a bitter herbal elixir with tonic and therapeutic qualities. As a token of gratitude for his support, in 1859, the friars handed the recipe to Averna, and in 1868 he started the production for his household guests.

PRODUCT: Amaro Averna

NOTES: A rich, full character with cola, licorice, vanilla, and cinnamon. The bitterness is balanced by stewy, rich fruit flavors and a hint of citrus. The botanicals are steeped in the base liquor before caramel is added. Wine Enthusiast's tasting notes: "An initial aroma of bittersweet dark chocolate, orange peel, and herbs; air contact stimulates scents of flowers, jasmine, bark, forest, honey, and very light quinine. The palate entry is intensely sweet and floral; at midpalate the taste profile turns cocoa-like with notes of citrus rind, molasses, brown sugar, and grass. Concludes sweet, thick, and luscious." 32% ABV

Barona, Italy

No information is available at the time of this printing.

PRODUCTS: Barona Bianco Vermouth, Barona Extra Dry Vermouth, Barona Rosso Vermouth

Bodegas Martinez Lacuesta S.A., Haro, Spain

www.martinezlacuesta.com/

Established in La Rioja at Haro, in 1895, by Don Félix Martínez Lacuesta, Bodegas Martinez Lacuesta was almost an overnight success throughout Spain. The country's fourth oldest registered winery, the company began exporting its wine portfolio first to Cuba in 1909 and a year later to the United States. It began vermouth production in 1937.

PRODUCT: Vermut Lacuesta Reserva

NOTES: Botanicals are macerated in white wine, which is then aged in American oak barrels. When matured, a base white wine, sugar, caramel, and spirit are added. The oak imbues this Spanish classic with a deep brown color and hints of vanilla. Like many of the Spanish vermouths the flavor has hints of spiced pumpkin. The overall character is closer to an amber vermouth than a sweet vermouth. 15% ABV.

Boisset, Nuits-Saint-Georges, France

www.boisset.fr

The story of St Raphaël apéritif begins, in 1830, when Dr. Adémar Juppet of Lyon almost lost his eyesight while trying to develop a cinchona apéritif, working late into the night in dim light. He prayed to the archangel Raphael who, in the Bible, had restored sight to Tobias. After he finalised his recipe, his eyesight improved and he dedicated his new drink to the angel. Originally sold in pharmacies as a tonic emphasizing the virtues of cinchona, this quinquina became a commercial success when, in 1890, Juppet's son Pierre trademarked the brand and marketed the beverage on an international scale. Recently, it has been re-branded, de-emphasizing the quinquina and highlighting the aperitif qualities.

PRODUCT: St Raphaël Rouge Aperitif

NOTES: Made from red mistelle and a heat maceration of cinchona, bitter orange peel, vanilla bean, cocoa beans, and a number of other botanicals. Sweet and bitter with spicy notes. 14.9% ABV

PRODUCT: St Raphaël Doré Aperitif

NOTES: Made from white mistelle and a heat maceration of cinchona, bitter orange peel, vanilla bean, cocoa beans, and a number of other botanicals. Amber-coloured, soft bodied with elegant spicy notes. 14.9% ABV

Bosca S.p.A., Canelli, Italy

www.bosca.it/

PRODUCT: Amaro Cora

NOTES: Brighter and sharper than a sweet vermouth, with distinctive citrus peel notes and cinnamon, Amaro Cora was the original vermouth component in the Torino-Milano cocktail and was exported to the Americas as early as 1838. 26% ABV

OTHER PRODUCTS: Vermouth Bosca Rosso, Cora Vermouth Rosso, Cora Vermouth Bianco

Byrrh, Perpignan, France

www.pernod.fr/english/marques/aperitifs_viniques/byrrh.html

Created in 1886, Byrrh was developed by itinerant drapers Pallade and Violet Simon, who wanted to create a cinchona-based apéritif wine. The resulting product was initially marketed as a health drink or tonic. This was because the local apéritif producers were not happy with new competition. The brothers re-branded the drink as a health drink to get around this problem, and it was sold in pharmacies. The Second World War initiated a decline in sales for Byrrh. Aided by tax benefits, natural sweet wines such as Banyuls, Muscat de Frontignan and Rivesaltes superseded Byrrh, which went out of fashion. In 1977 the family business, divided by strife, was acquired by Pernod-Ricard, which still produces the beverage at its Perpignan facility, which was designed by Gustav Eiffel. Recently, Byrrh has been rising in popularity once again.

PRODUCT: Byrrh

NOTES: A wine-based aperitif, Byrrh has a specific quinine character. Made from Carignan and Grenache grape varieties that are grown in the Roussillon hillsides, this aromatized wine is often served with a splash of crème de cassis and a lemon twist. 17% ABV

PRODUCT: Byrrh Rare Assemblage

This apéritif is made from selected vintage Catalan wines which are steeped with cinchona and other botanicals in cellars located in Thuir, France and aged in small oak barrels for approximately 10 years. This produces an intense and full aroma with developing notes of candied red fruit. The wine possesses well blended tannins, sustained by subtle quinine notes. Fine wine-based ingredients develop aromas of dried fruit, with hints of chocolate and spices. The finish carries notes of vanilla-flavoured coffee and toast. 17% ABV

Campagnia Florio, Palermo, Italy

Dating back to the early 19th century, Florio Amaro took its name from its consumers as it was originally reserved for the sailors on ships owned by the Florio shipping company which plied a number of transoceanic routes from Sicily.

PRODUCT: Florio Amaro

NOTES: An infusion of thirteen botanicals aged for at least eighteen months in wood, this amaro has a distinct bitter citrus aroma and rich mouthfeel. 32% ABV

Cappellano Winery, Gabutti, Italy

The Cappellano family has produced wine in the Barolo region since 1870. Giuseppe Cappellano, a pharmacist in Serralunga d'Alba, undertook the creation of a digestive. This elixir soon became famous amongst the Piemontese bourgeoisie and much appreciated by the house of Savoy, who served it at royal banquets not only as a digestive, but also as an apéritif and as a dessert wine to accompany chocolate.

PRODUCT: Cappellano Barolo Chinato

NOTES: This chinato is an infusion of Barolo with quinine bark, clove, wormwood and cinnamon plus a small amount of cane sugar. It portrays an aroma of rose and anise with cherry, orange peel and subtle hints of green herbs.

Danish Distillers, Limited, Dalby, Denmark

www.gammeldansk.dk

Gammel Dansk was one of the original products produced by De Danske Spritfabrikker that was founded in 1881 by C.F. Tietgen and C.A. Olsen.

PRODUCT: Gammel Dansk Bitter Dram

NOTES: Angelica, rowan berries, star anise, nutmeg, ginger, laurel, gentian, seville orange peel, and cinnamon are in the blend. The classic Gammel Dansk (which translates to "Old Danish") Bitter Dram was first sold in Danish groceries in 1964. In both taste and appearance it is true to the original recipe. The secret behind the special bitter taste lies in the particular measures of the 28 different botanicals. 38% ABV

Davide Campari-Milano S.p.A., Sesto San Giovanni, Italy

www.camparigroup.com

Gruppo Campari traces its beginnings back to 1860, with the birth of its flagship brand Campari. [HISTORY OF CAMPARI]

PRODUCT: Aperol Aperitivo

NOTES: The Barbieri brothers of Padova originated Aperol in 1919. Purchased in the 1990s by Barbero 1891 S.p.A., Aperol then entered Gruppo Campari's portfolio.

Produced using 16 ingredients including gentian, orange essence, rhubarb and cinchona. Wine Enthusiast notes that it has: "Sophisticated and delightful aromas of tangerine and rhubarb. The palate entry is delightfully citrusy and sweet; the midpalate phase offers just enough herbal bitterness to balance. Ends up refreshing, orangey sweet and delectably herbal." 11% ABV

PRODUCT: Campari Bitter

NOTES: Gaspari Campari invented Campari Bitter in Novara, in 1860. The company's first production plant was opened, in 1904, in Sesto San Giovanni. At that time they also began exporting to overseas markets. Wine Enthusiast notes that: "The nosing passes find earthy/woodsy scents of brambles/vines, moss, forest floor and stones. The palate entry owns a unique tree bark-like taste that's oddly attractive; the midpalate stage features pungent flavors of ashes, roots, quinine, honey, citrus peels and earth." 24% ABV

PRODUCT: Cynar Carciofo Amaro

TASTING NOTES: Cynar is an artichoke based bitter that infuses 13 botanicals. It was launched in 1952 as a digestive, served after dinner, however its similarity to sweet vermouth makes it a versatile cocktail ingredient. In Europe it is most commonly served with orange juice, but can also be added to beer or used as a vermouth replacement in a Manhattan. The flavour is rich and bittersweet, balsamic character typical of a traditional rich red vermouth with hints of lychee and coppery sharpness. 16.5 ABV

PRODUCT: Biancosarti

NOTES: Biancosarti, primarily marketed in Italy, is an apéritif infused from a variety of botanicals, especially citrus and flowers. It has a distinct vanilla flavour with citrus, herbaceous and bitter earthy notes. 28% ABV

PRODUCT: Amaro Diesus del Frate

NOTES: The well-known bitterness of this amaro combines gentian, angelica, sandalwood, lemon, Colombo, galanga, artichoke, elder, dittany crettico, aloe head, china calisaya, clary sage, cardamom, marjoram gentle, blessed thistle, peppermint, nutmeg yarrow, hyssop, centaury, mandarin, bitter orange, juniper, anise, chamomile, waxy mountain, wormwood, grains of paradise, Pontic wormwood, hops flowers, wormwood, zedoaria enula bell, mountain thyme, iris, ginger, cinnamon, Ceylon and Chinese rhubarb. 18% ABV

OTHER PRODUCTS: Riccadonna Bianco Vermouth, Riccadonna Rosso Vermouth

Distilleria Caffo di Limbadi, Limbadi, Italy

www.distilleriacaffo.com

After years of experience trading and managing distilleries, Giuseppe Caffo bought an old distillery, in 1915, in Santa

Venerina, Sicily. He initially produced wine-based spirits, alcohol and derivatives, but then he introduced a few herbal liqueurs based on old recipes, which is where he met with his greatest success.

PRODUCT: Vecchio Amaro del Capo

NOTES: This herb based liqueur is based on an old Calabrese recipe, infusing 29 local botanicals in alcohol, including bitter orange, sweet orange, liquorice, mandarin, chamomile and juniper. 35% ABV

PRODUCT: Caffo Finocchietto

NOTES: An amaro whose primary element is fennel, Finocchietto also infuses a number of other botanicals in spirit. 28% ABV

PRODUCT: Nocino del Monte Poro

NOTES: Green Clabrian walnuts are the featured element in this amaro, which also includes other botanicals steeped in spirit. 35% ABV

Distilleria Fratelli Ramazotti S.p.A., Milno, Italy

www.ramazzotti.it/

Ausano Ramazzotti opened his first café in Milano, in 1815, featuring his Amaro Ramazzotti as the signature drink.

PRODUCT: Amaro Ramazzotti

NOTES: A tonic liqueur that steeps 33 botanicals including gentian root, rhubarb, cinnamon, and Sicilian orange peel in spirit. 30% ABV

Distillerie Dr. Cav. F. Peloni S.p.A., Bormio, Italy

amarobraulio.it

In 1875 the botanist Dottore Francesco Peloni developed Amaro Braulio in Bormio, in Italy's Lombardy region.

PRODUCT: Braulio Amaro Alpino

NOTES: The botanicals in this unique Amaro are exclusively fresh herbs, plus spring water from the Valtellina mountain region. The botanicals are dried in the fresh mountain air and then steeped in spring water and alcohol for a month. Strained, the finished liquid is matured for 2 years in oak barrels. Full-bodied herbaceousness, balanced bitter and sweetness, rich and round. 21% ABV

Distillerie de la Salers, Montaignac St-Hippolyte, France

www.gentiane-salers.com

Alfred Labounoux studied distillation in Bordeaux and earned his living as an itinerant distiller, renting his services to Alsatian farmers. Eventually he opened his own facility in Corrèze, specializing in making kirsch and a variation, guignolet. With growing interest in cinchona and gentian apéritifs in the marketplace, Labounoux developed, in 1885, the first gentian liqueur, Salers Gentiane.

PRODUCT: Salers Gentiane

NOTES: The product was named after the village of Salers Labounoux. The surrounding mountains are the source for the gentian used in its manufacture. Yellow gentian and other botanicals are macerated in spirit and aged in oak barrels. It is produced in 16% (yellow cap), 20% (red cap), and 25% (green cap) ABV versions. Salers Gentiane "green cap" portrays notes of citrus, red fruits, and cocoa, which is less bitter than its counterparts.

PRODUCT: Eau-de-vie de Gentiane

NOTES: Yellow gentian roots are fermented in heated cellars for 6 weeks before they are distilled to 20% ABV and then redistilled to 65% ABV before final dilution to 43% ABV.

Distillerie Societe J. Chatel & Cie, Saint-Denis, Réunion

www.groupechatel.com

No information is available at the time of this printing. Possibly no longer produced.

PRODUCTS: Chatel Vermouth

Distillerie de la Suze, France

www.suze.com

Distillerie Rousseau, Laurens et Moureaux located in Maisons-Alfort dates back to 1795 and even at this early date the company was making a gentian apéritif with a wine base, the precursor to Suze. The now-familiar recipe was invented, in 1885, by Fernand Moureaux who originally called his recipe Le Picotin, a distillate of gentian roots that was unique at that time. Widely marketed throughout France, by 1889, the product became known as Moureaux Suze, named after his sister-in-law Susanne Jaspert. (There is some controversy as to whether the drink recipe actually originated in Switzerland, near the River Suze, by a local who sold the recipe to Moureaux, and took its name from the river instead.) The distinctive signature amber bottle was designed, in 1896, by Henri Porte. Success and rapid growth demanded the establishment, in 1922, of Distillerie Suze.

PRODUCT: Suze

NOTES: Yellow gentian comprises over a third of the total botanicals by weight used in this distillate, which offers a dry, earthy, bitter-sweet character with subtle finishing notes. 15% ABV

Ditta Bortolo Nardini S.p.A., Bassano del Grappa, Italy

www.nardini.it

Bortolo Nardini—already an expert in the art of distillation—left his home town of Segonzano, in 1779, to open his distillery and "grapperia" in Bassano at the entrance to a famous bridge designed by Palladio on the Brenta river.

PRODUCT: Nardini Amaro Liqueur

NOTES: Nardini amaro appeals to tawny port drinkers. The botanicals emerge primarily on the finish, while the mouth and nose encounter mocha, toffee, and baking spices. A grain alcohol base is infused with botanicals including bitter orange, peppermint, and gentian. Intense dark chocolate colour. Bitter with an excellent fruit and herbal balance. A fresh impact of mint, the gentian offers a pleasurable finish of liquorice. 31% ABV

Ditta Silvio Meletti S.R.L., Ascoli Piceno, Italy

www.meletti.it

Silvio Meletti was raised in a poor family and soon quit his studies to work with his mother at her small store in which she sold a home-made anise liquor. Silvio learned his mother's technique and recipes and started studying French essays on distillation. After several experiments, in 1870, he enhanced the recipe and distillation technique that is still used today to obtain the Anisetta Meletti. He met with such success, he began developing other liqueurs.

PRODUCT: Amaro Meletti

NOTES: There is a hint of floral, primarily violet. There is some saffron presence and a white pepper note that builds through the finish. The botanicals are introduced through a cold maceration process similar to coffee percolation. 32% ABV

Dubonnet Company, Bardstown KY

www.doyoudubonnet.com

From its origins with the French Foreign Legion to the legions of modern mixologists still using it today, Dubonnet Rouge Apéritif Wine has been a staple on the cocktail landscape since its introduction in 1846. Created by Parisian chemist/wine merchant Joseph Dubonnet as a means to make quinine more palatable for the soldiers in malaria-ridden parts of North Africa, Dubonnet's mix of fortified wine and botanicals, including cinchona, is a recipe that has earned it legendary status in the world of sophisticated drinks.

PRODUCT: Dubonnet Rouge

NOTES: Wine Enthusiast notes: "Tawny color like an old Burgundy. Bouquet is vinegary and tart, with nuances of pine, underripe grapes and fruit stone. Fresh and clean on palate; thin flavor displays tastes of tart cranberry." 14.8% ABV

PRODUCT: Dubonnet Blanc

NOTES: Comparable to a light sherry, this aperitif wine has soft, sweet floral and citrus notes that accentuate rather than masking the base wine. 14.8% ABV

PRODUCT: Dubonnet Gold

NOTES: Medium-sweet with light honey and citrus notes. 14.8% ABV

Emilio Miró Salvat S.A., Reus, Spain

www.mirosalvat.com

The company was founded, in 1957, in Spain's Tarragona province. The Miró family has been growing Grenache and Macabeo grapes for generations.

PRODUCT: Vermouth Miró Rojo

NOTES: No tastings notes are available at the time of this printing. 15% ABV

PRODUCT: Vermouth Miró Blanco

NOTES: No tastings notes are available at the time of this printing. 15% ABV

PRODUCT: Vermouth Miró Extra Dry

NOTES: No tastings notes are available at the time of this printing. 15% ABV

PRODUCT: Vermouth Casero

NOTES: No tastings notes are available at the time of this printing. 15% ABV

PRODUCT: Vermouth Miró Piramidal

NOTES: No tastings notes are available at the time of this printing. 16% ABV

PRODUCT: Vermouth Miró Rojo Reserva

NOTES: No tastings notes are available at the time of this printing. 16% ABV

PRODUCT: Vermouth Miró Reserva Black Label

NOTES: No tastings notes are available at the time of this printing. 16% ABV

PRODUCT: Vermut Farlatti Rojo

NOTES: No tastings notes are available at the time of this printing. 15% ABV

PRODUCT: Vermut Farlatti Blanco

NOTES: No tastings notes are available at the time of this printing. 15% ABV

Felice Bisleri & C. S.A., Italy

Felice Bisleri was born in Gerolanuova. He established the Felice Bislieri & Co. chemical laboratory in Milano, developing the successful "Ferro-China Bislieri", an amaro made as an alcohol infusion of cinchona, botanicals, and iron salts.

PRODUCT: Ferro China Bisleri

NOTES: An herbal amaro. 21% ABV

Fratelli Branca Distillerie, Milano, Italy

www.branca.it

Bernardino Branca founded the company, in 1845, and invented Fernet-Branca bitter. By 1907, DIno Brance took over the copmany and expended operations throughout Europe and North America. He opened new distilleries in Buenos Aires, St Louis, Chiasso, and New York. The company acquired the Carpano company in 2001.

PRODUCT: Carpano Antica Formula Vermouth

NOTES: A huge profile. Menthol, tobacco, tar, prune and deep citrus peel. Round and full, clove and cinnamon, and cardamon. Remarkably balanced. Grapefruit peel finish. The Beverage Testing Institute notes: "Deep mahogany color. Cascading aromas of cinnamon bark, cola nut, honeycomb, tart dried cherries and oranges, and raisin nut compote with a supple fruity full body and a long, vanilla and medicinal root and smoky bark finish." 16.5% ABV

PRODUCT: Fernet-Branca

NOTES: In 1845, Bernardino Branca created Fernet-Branca. Made from 27 botanicals, including aloes, gentian, rhubarb, myrrh, red cinchona bark, rhubarb, wormwood, bay, echinacea, ginseng, St John's wort, sage, peppermint, cardamom, saffron and other exotic spices such as galangal and zedoary. The fragrance of oak barrels, perfectly balanced blend of flavors matured for twelve months. Beverage Testing Institute notes: "Dark brown color. Deep aromas of peppermint leaf, chicory, unsweetened chocolate, forest flowers and herb jump from the glass and follow thorough on a supple entry to a dryish full body with layers of cocoa-mint, peppery spice, sandalwood, and bitter roots and medicinal herbs. Finishes with a long, polished wood, peppermint oil, nutshell and bitter root fade." 45% ABV

PRODUCT: Fernet Branca-Menta

NOTES: Brancamenta was created in the mid-1960s, when the trendiest youngsters began asking for a glass of Fernet-Branca with a hint of mint syrup, thus unconsciously giving birth to a new tonic and refreshing drink. It has light-brown color, balanced but intense flavor, a refined accent. The unique blend of mints from the Piedmonte with over 30 botanicals gives the distinctive and pleasant aroma. 45% ABV

PRODUCT: Punt e Mes

NOTES: Made by the Carpano family from 1870 until 2001 (when it was purchased by Fratelli Branca), Punt e Mes is darker, richer, and slightly more bitter than sweet vermouths. The flavour is comparable to Carpano Antica with a splash of Campari.

It has been said that back in 1870 a stock exchange agent caught up in a debate with some colleagues at Bottega Carpano, asked for the vermouth laced with half -dose of china bitters, after the Piedmontese expression "Punt e Mes". The peculiar origin of the new name was soon enhanced by a curious habit introduced by Carpano regular customers—to ask for Punt e Mes with a simple signal, a the raised thumb up (one Punt) and a clean, horizontal line in the air with the hand open (a Mes).

OTHER PRODUCTS: Carpano Classico Vermut, Carpano Bianco Vermut

Fratelli Martini Secondo Luigi, S.p.A., Cossano Belbo, Italy

www.fratellimartini.it

Established in the Langhe region of Piedmont by two brothers, Secondo and Luigi Martini in 1947 who were primarily interested in producing traditional still and sparkling regional wines. The company grew rapidly in the 1970s with the second generation of the family driving an ambitious expansion of their lines, including: Casa Sant'Orsola, Canti, 35° parallelo, Collezione Marchesini, Il Cortigiano, I Firmati, and the Versasi vermouths.

PRODUCT: Versasi Vermouth Extra Dry

NOTES: The flavour profile is shaped by cardamom, cinnamon, allspice, marjoram, and chamomile. 14.8% ABV
PRODUCT: Versasi Vermouth Sweet
NOTES: The flavour profile is shaped by orange peel, cinnamon, allspice, and vanilla. 14.8% ABV

Fratelli Vignale Nicola e Battista S.r.l., Genoa, Italy

The company was founded, in 1892, by Nicola Vignale in Genoa.

PRODUCT: Amaro Santa maria al Monte
NOTES: The Santa Maria al Monte is perhaps the most extreme example of alpine herbal amaro. This amaro is deeply complex with loads of spicy detail in the mouth and a long, bitter and mint finish. 40% ABV

Fratelli Gancia & C. S.p.A., Canelli, Italy

www.gancia.it
Founded in 1850 by Carlo Gancia, this producer is best known for creating the first Italian sparkling wine.

PRODUCT: Vermouth Gancia Rosso
NOTES: Particularly rich and intense fragrance obtrained from the extract and maceration of herbs and spices a wine

base alcohol solution. Sweet, aromatic and pleasantly dry and persistent. 16% ABV

PRODUCT: Vermouth Gancia Biano

NOTES: This bianco vermouth leads with a big aroma of dry and sweet spices. The flavor is herbaceous, filled with vanilla, cinnamon and clove, and full-bodied. Particularly delicate and intense fragrance resulting from the blending of the herb and spice extract in the alcohol base to the wine base. Sweet, full, and velvety. 14.8% ABV

PRODUCT: Vermouth Gancia Dry

NOTES: Particularly delicate and intense fragrance resulting from the blending of the herb and spice extract in the alcohol base to the wine base. Dry and delicate taste with a slightly bitter and persistent aftertaste. 18% ABV

PRODUCT: Americano Apéritif

NOTES: Americano Gancia features wormwood and gentian, the sweet and bitter taste of orange with all the freshness and magic of wine and oriental spices. Divided into three phases. The most neutral wines are chosen which are better amalgamated with the herbs and spices selected for mixing. The herbs, some local (wormwood, cerea, sweet and bitter orange) and some exotic (cinnamon, sandalwood, cloves, nutmeg, china bark), are chosen and amalgamated to obtain a liquid with an alcohol content of 30°. This liquid is then mixed into the wine with sugar and extracts, and is filtered and refined in stainless steel tanks. 14.5% ABV

Giulio Cocchi Spumanti S.r.l., Italy

www.cocchi.it

Giulio Cocchi was working in Florence's most popular bar, located in Piazza del Duomo. But in the late 1800s he moved to Asti and opened his own business as a distiller and sparkling wine maker. In the late 1970s, the Cocchi business became the property of the Bava family that modernized the production and relaunched the Barolo Chinato Cocchi.

PRODUCT: Barolo Chinato Cocchi

NOTES: Barolo Chinato is a special wine produced with DOCG Barolo, flavoured with quinine bark, rhubarb and gentian, of which extracts are obtained through maceration at room temperature, with a final addition of spices including selected cardamom seeds. Created in Piedmont in the last century, it quickly became popular because of its attractive bitter-sweet taste and above all because of the Barolo name, which firmly put it into place as a prestigious product in the quinine flavoured alcohol range. Giulio Cocchi invented this unique recipe in 1891. 16.5% ABV

PRODUCT: Cocchi Aperitivo Americano

NOTES: Giulio Cocchi's original Americano recipe was born in 1891. White wine is aromatized with botanicals and produced in limited quantities that are matured for a year. 16.5% ABV

PRODUCT: Cocchi Storico Vermouth di Torino

NOTES: To celebrate the 120th anniversary of the House of Cocchi, the company resumed production of Giulio Cocchi's original recipe Vermouth di Torino, previously produced in 1891. The flavor profile is unmistakably of Cocchi, with rich and vibrant notes of citrus, cocoa, rhubarb and a balanced bitter undertone. 16% ABV

Karlovarská Becherovka a.s., Karlovy Vary, Czech Republic

Josef Vitus Becher traded in spices and colonial goods in his shop "At the Three Skylarks". He also began producing spirits in 1794, when he rented a stillhouse in the town, a place to execute his distillation experiements. Josef's business was taken over in 1838 by his son Johann Nepomuk Becher.

PRODUCT: Becherovka

NOTES:Becherovka is an herbal bitters flavoured with anise seed, cinnamon, and approximately 32 other botancials. 38% ABV

Kedem, Marlboro NY, USA

www.royalwines.com, www.kedemwinery.com

Launched in 1958 by Eugene Herzog, a Czechoslovakian immigrant to the United States. He arrived with his family at the time of the communist takeover in his home country where his family had been making wine for eight generations. The Kedem Winery produces a wide variety of certified kosher wines in Marlboro, New York, up the Hudson River from New York City.

PRODUCT: Kedem Dry Kosher Vermouth

NOTES: Light botanicals, rounded dry character with high alcohol presence, crisp and clean finish. 18% ABV

PRODUCT: Kedem Sweet Kosher Vermouth

NOTES: Sweet and slightly honeyed with caramel, citrus and spice, rich mouthfeel. 17% ABV

La Canellese, Canelli, Italy

www.lacanellese.it/azienda_eng.html

Producers in the town of Canelli claim to have given birth to the first Spumantes, sparkling wines. During the 1950s, La Canellese added vermouths to its portfolio of wine products.

PRODUCT: La Canellese Vermouth Bianco

NOTES: Straw-coloured aperitif with moderate alcohol content. It is produced from selected white wines, grape alcohol, and sugar. It is enriched in flavour by the infusion of herbs such as wormwood, coriander, and sage. 16% ABV

PRODUCT: La Canellese Vermouth di Torino

NOTES: Produced from selected white wines, alcohol and sugar. It is enriched in flavour by the infusion of herbs such as wormwood, coriander and sage. It differs from the White Vermouth with its amber colour and stronger aroma. 16% ABV

PRODUCT: La Canellese Vermouth Chinato

NOTES: Produced from selected white wines, alcohol and sugar. It is enriched in flavour by the infusion of herbs such as wormwood, coriander and sage. It has a deep amber colour, and differs from the red vermouth as it has a distinctly sharp, dry bittered character. 16% ABV

PRODUCT: La Canellese Barolo Chinato

NOTES: Based on Barolo DOCG wine, pure calisaya, cloves, cinnamon and cardamom are steeped in the base wine.

PRODUCT: La Canellese Vino Aromatizzato

NOTES: Full-bodied Barbera wine is macerated with cinchona, gentian root, cardamom seeds, calamus root, vanilla and clove. Deep red in colour and heavily scented, it has a strong, gentle and harmonic taste.

PRODUCT: La Canellese Amaro San

NOTES: A lightly bitter apéritif, based on wine and aromatic herbs.

PRODUCT: La Canellese Americano

NOTES: A young, modern apéritif based on wine with a suitable sweet and bitter orange character, flavoured with various herbs. 16% ABV

Likörfabrik Peter Busch GmbH & Co. KG

www.killepitsch.de

Hans Müller-Schlösser, creator of the "Schneider Wibbel" and Willi Busch, an old master of traditional customs came up with Killeptisch during World War II. The story goes that sometime toward the end of the war a promise was made to celebrate a new beginning with the invention of a new drink. "If they don't 'kill' us, we have a chance to 'pitsch' a few more." It finally went into commercial production in 1955. That year the small, well-stocked Bar Et Kabüffke opened on Flinger Strasse, Hans came upon his friend Willi on the opening night. "Hey, Willy, what came of the idea Killepitsch! I bet you've forgotten all about it!" he taunted him. "No," said Willi. "I had not forgotten—it's been ready for ages Here it is. Cheers Mmm, it smells delicious, like a garden herb, strong, not too vague, not too bitter And it must be good for the digestion. It slips down a treat! "

PRODUCT: Killepitsch

NOTES: A kräterlikör made with 90 fruits, berries, and botanicals, it was a regional speciality in Düsseldorf that is now distributed worldwide. With a hint of molasses and menthol. 42% ABV

La Distillerie Bonal, St Laurent du Pont, France

No details available at the time of this printing.

PRODUCT: Bonal Gentiane Quina

NOTES: Since 1865, this apéritif has been produced in St-Laurent-du-Pont. Popular with sportsmen, Bonal was an early sponsor of the Tour de France. A basis of a mistelle grapes (grape must whose fermentation is stopped by the addition of alcohol), quinine and gentian, Bonal is a bitter-sweet deep brown coloured drink, which in general character is not far from sweet vermouth. Gentian, cinchona, bitter orange, and other botanicals are macerated in a mistelle for an undisclosed period of time before spirit is added. Tasting notes from Post Prohibition (www.postprohibition.com): "Bonal Gentiane Quina has a reddish brown color and an upfront smell of prunes or raisins. Upon sipping I first noticed flavors of raisins/grapes. The mid-palette contains the bitter elements from the gentian root and cinchona. It finishes sweet with grapes and hints of cherry and licorice." 16% ABV

Lillet Frères SA, Podensac, France

Brothers Paul and Raymond Lillet, distillers and merchants of wines and spirits, founded their company La Maison Lillet , in 1872, in Podensac, France. They were inspired by Father Kermann, a doctor who left Brazil at the beginning of Louis XVI's reign and settled in Bordeaux, where he produced liqueurs and aromatized wines from botanicals such as quinine. Introduced in 1895, Kina Lillet became very famous in France during the 1920s both because of its quality and its advertising campaigns. It was exported throughout Europe, and Lillet Dry was produced for the British market. Sales rose in Africa, followed by its introduction into the United States. Lillet Rouge, created in the 1960s, was specially developed for the American market. Kina Lillet was renamed Lillet Blanc in the 1960s, after Lillet Rouge was introduced. Because its original bitter character did not fit with changing public tastes, the company reformulated Lillet Blanc in 1985 with reduced quinine content while maintaining the unique dry citrus character.

PRODUCT: Lillet Blanc Quinquina

NOTES: A burst of Seville orange gives way to sanguinello, pine, menthol, dry fruit, and heavy minerals. Wine Enthusiast notes: "The rounded bouquet features tropical fruit notes of banana and guava, smells of ripe grapes and kiwi and a subtle spiciness. The palate entry is luscious, gently fruity and keenly acidic; midpalate flavors include kiwi, white grapes, raisins, and a vegetal quality. Finish is ripe, delicately spiced, and delicious." 17% ABV.

PRODUCT: Lillet Rouge Quinquina

NOTES: Wine Enthusiast notes: "Cherry-red color. Assertive bouquet of freshly picked grapes, black cherries, black raspberries, apricots and pepper keeps the olfactory sense focused. In the mouth, it behaves like a fat, chewy red from the sun-drenched south of France; tastes ambrosial and clean. Finishes short, mildly fruity and ripe." 17% ABV

Girolamo Luxardo S.p.A., Torreglia, Italy

www.luxardo.it

The Luxardo firm was founded, in 1821, in Zara, a port city on the Dalmatian coast (now part of the republic of Croatia) which had been, for more than six centuries, an integral part of the "Serenissima" republic of Venice. At the fall of the Venetian republic in 1797, Zara was designated the capital of the Kingdom of Dalmatia, under Austrian sovereignty. A citizen of Genoa, Girolamo Luxardo, was sent, in 1817, to Zara as consular representative of the Kingdom of Sardinia. His wife Maria Canevari dedicated herself to making liqueurs at home. She was especially interested in perfecting a "rosolio maraschino", a liqueur produced in Dalmatia since medieval times and often made in convents. The liqueur she produced was of such high quality that it claimed the attention not only of family and friends but of serious connoisseurs. Girolamo founded a distillery, in 1821, to produce her maraschino liqueur.

PRODUCT: Luxardo Amaro Abano

NOTES: The herbs in this amaro grow wild in the Euganean Hills and are additionally enhanced with cardamom, cinnamon and bitter orange peel. Amaro Abano is a medium bitter, extremely popular in Italy, especially in the Veneto. 30% ABV

PRODUCT: Luxardo Amaro Abano Dry

NOTES: A drier digestive liqueur obtained from a carefully selected blend of various bitter herbs. 32% ABV

PRODUCT: Luxardo Bitter

NOTES: A Campari-type apéritif in the Luxardo style that was first made in 1885. The character stems from the infusion of several herbs and spices such as sweet orange, bitter orange, rhubarb, mint, marjoram and thyme. 18% ABV

PRODUCT: Luxardo Fernet

NOTES: A strongly bitter amaro, Luxardo Fernet undergoes prolonged infusion of herbs and spices such as licorice, condurango, cardamom, cinnamon, enzian, and saffron. Luxardo has produced this Fernet since 1889 is known for its ability to stimulate the digestive juices. 45% ABV

PRODUCT: Aperitivo Luxardo

NOTES: Similar to Aperol, Aperitivo Luxardo is the result of a well balanced infusion of herbs, roots and citrus. 11% ABV

PRODUCT: Liquore St Antonio

NOTES: The unique specialty of Padova, Saint Anthony liqueur is prepared by an infusion of rare herbs including angelica, achillea, galangal root and bitter oranges. 40% ABV

Maison Dolin & Cie, Chambéry, France

www.dolin.fr

Maison Dolin & Cie is the last remaining producer of Vermouth de Chambéry, which in 1932, earned France's only AOC in the category. Vermouth de Chambéry was first developed, in 1821, by Joseph Chavasse, whose son-in-law Ferdinand Dolin inherited the recipe, in 1842, and founded the company. A hallmark of Vermouth de Chambéry was the creation of the Blanc (aka: Bianco) style.

PRODUCT: Dolin Dry Vermouth

NOTES: Infused with 17 botanicals on an ugni blanc wine base. CLASS Magazine notes: "Clear, pale golden hue with slight green tinge. Fresh lychee and grape juice nose with aromas of bark, almond, citrus fruit, pine forest and faint hairspray. White wine palate with white wine vinegar, génépi (alpine plant) and pine and salty seaweed flavours. Fresh, clean, slightly acidic, spicy slightly oxidized white wine finish." 17% ABV

PRODUCT: Dolin Blanc Vermouth

NOTES: Infused with 33 botanicals and lightly sweetened on an ugni blanc wine base. CLASS Magazine notes: "Clear, pale golden hue with slight green tinge. Spicy bark nose with menthol, sea salt, faint pine and old lady's perfume. Delicate, slightly sweet palate balanced by white wine acidity with white fruit (grape, pear, ripe pineapple), pine, citrus fruit and floral (elderflower) flavours. Well balanced bitter-sweet-acidic finish with lasting elderflower and citrus flavours." 16% ABV

PRODUCT: Dolin Rouge Vermouth

NOTES: Infused with with 35 botanicals and lightly sweetened on an ugni blanc wine base. CLASS Magazine notes: "Clear, dark copper, reddy-brown. Sarsaparilla and citrus zest nose with stewed fruits, quince, and Christmas spices (clove and cinnamon). Perfectly balanced, bitter-sweet sarsaparilla, herbaceous, citrus zest, prune/stewed fruit, quinine and cigar tobacco palate with light spice. Bitter citrus notes lead the tobacco, citrus zest and quinine finish." 16% ABV

PRODUCT: Dolin Chambéryzette Apéritif

NOTES: Dolin Blanc vermouth additionally flavoured with wild alpine strawberries. Reputedly, this apéritif was first introduction during the 1800s to British tourists visiting the area to take the wateres. One of the first of these visitors to appreciate this rare vermouth was Queen Victoria. 16% ABV

PRODUCT: Dolin Genepi

NOTES: A maceration of genepy, sugar, and spirit with 63 other botanicals, a stalk of genepy is placed inside each bottle.

Maraska, Zadar, Croatia

www.maraska.hr

The company website includes a detailed and vibrantly illustrated historical timeline dating from 1338 up to the present day. Unfortunately, all text is offered in Hungarian only.

PRODUCT: Amaro Zara

NOTES: Amaro Zara is an herbal liqueur, developed in 1821, that combines a variety of aromatic botanicals to produce a distinctive and rich, slightly bitter taste. 30% ABV

Marcarini Azienda Agricola, La Morra, italy

www.marcarini.it

A splendid, unique digestive and dessert wine, the Barolo Chinato traces its origins to the heart of the Barolo region toward the end of the 1800s.

PRODUCT: Marcarini Chinato

NOTES: This is a Barolo Chinato that is infused with chinabark, rhubarb and other botanicals. Amber-colored and with ruby-red reflections. Its spicy, intense and persistent nose and the bittersweet taste of the China bark are enhanced by its ageing in oak barrels. 16% ABV

Martini & Rossi S.p.A., Pessione, Italy

www.martini.com

Headed by Carlo Re, Distilleria Nazioale de Spirito de Vino in San Salvatore Monferrato established a vermouth production division in 1849. It was successful enough that by the 1860s, the company moved production to its own facility at Pessione. With expansion came the need for fresh leadership. Company director Alessandro Martini, vintner Luigi Rossi, and accountant Teofilo Sola, who took over the firm in 1863 and renamed it Martini, Sola & Cia. With medals from both Dublin and Paris international exhibitions as well as a royal warrant under its belt, by 1868, the company began exportation to the United States. With this move, Martini, Sola & Cia became the first Italian company to commercially produce and market Vermouth di Torino throughout the world.

When the Sola family sold out its shares, in 1879, the company changes its name to Martini & Rossi. The term "Martini" was synonymous with Italian vermouth and Vermouth di Torino with customers and bartenders outside of Italy. Then, in 1882, Harry Johnson published the first recipes for a Martini and a Bradford à la Martini. From then until today, the family of Vermouth cocktails exploded. The company's influence on the development of the cocktail is discussed in depth in the cocktail chapter.

PRODUCT: Martini Rosso Vermouth

NOTES: Coppery rich reddish brown in colour. Vatted in neutral stainless steel to preserve the flavour of the botanicals rather than modifying them with oak, it has good intensity. Elegant with distinct dry straw, rich honey and bitter herbal notes to the nose. Flavour leads with a distinctive bitter-sweet character well-balanced with soft spices and dry meadow notes, leading to an assertively crisp and bitter finish. 15% ABV

PRODUCT: Martini Bianco Vermouth

NOTES: Very pale white-gold colour. Launched in 1910, this vermouth is pleasant and elegant, with sweet hints of vanilla on a foundation of grasses and lemon with sweet floral notes. 15% ABV

PRODUCT: Martini Extra Dry Vermouth

NOTES: Glints of light straw and faint gold in the colour. Introduced on New Year's Day in 1900, this vermouth is vibrant and harmonic, with delicate rumours of raspberries and lemon on a foundation of grass notes. Rich and dry on the palate. Sophisticated. 15% ABV

PRODUCT: Martini Rosato Vermouth

NOTES: The colour of a deep rich rosé. A balanced floral nose with hints of pastille and lemon. The taste leads with bittered rose then into wild strawberry (fraises des bois), with meyer lemon and grapefruit in the finish. 15% ABV

PRODUCT: Martini Gold Vermouth

NOTES: Spiced orange and powdered sugar on the nose. Soft bitter orange and light summer berries are countered with dry, bitter spices with vanilla rising in the finish. 18% ABV

PRODUCT: Martini Fiero Vermouth

NOTES: Colour of an aged rosé: deep blush with hints of copper. Pronounced sweet grapefruit nose underpinned with buttery vanilla and a hint of rosemary. Sanguinello (blood orange) is instantly apparent in the taste, with its rich, honeyed citrus character balanced to medium-dry with bitter herbal notes. 14.9% ABV

PRODUCT: Martini D'Oro

NOTES: An aperitif wine, it is not technically a vermouth. Rich gold colour. Seville orange, cinnamon and caramel on the nose. Sweet orange, soft vanilla, and rich bitter and savory herbaceousness provide a full and balanced flavour. 9% ABV

PRODUCT: Martini Bitter

NOTES: Brilliant raspberry red colour. Orange with a hint of pink grapefruit lead a chorus of herbal aromas. Balanced sweet and bitter underlie an assertive grapefruit and botanical bitter. It is concentrated and can be overwhelming straight. It is ideal iced or mixed. 25% ABV

PRODUCT: China Martini

NOTES: Bitter orange and sweet spices dominate the nose. The taste is balanced between bitter orange, dry bitter herbs with the character of wormwood, and light caramel. 31% ABV

Mast-Jägermeister SE, Wolfenbüttel, Germany

www.jagermeister.com

The term Jägermeister was introduced in Germany, in 1934, with the new Reichsjagdgesetz (Reich hunting law). The term was applied to senior civil service foresters and gamekeepers. When this herbal liqueur was introduced, in 1935, the name was already familiar to Germans. Curt Mast, the original distiller of Jägermeister, was an enthusiastic hunter.

PRODUCT: Jägermeister

NOTES: This kräuterlikör includes 56 botanicals including citrus peel, liquorice, anise, poppy seeds, saffron, ginger, juniper berries, and ginseng which are infused in water and alcohol for 2–3 days. Afterwards, this mixture is filtered and stored in oak barrels for about a year before it is filtered again, sweetened, fortified with additional spirit and water, filtered once more and then bottled. 35% ABV

Melchiorre Cinzano & Co, SA, Italy

This company is no longer in existence, but was the producer of Vermouth Melchior.

Montana-Perucchi S.A., Badalona-Barcelona, Spain

www.perucchi.info

Montana Perucchi, founded by Augustus Perucchi in 1876, has been making vermouth in Barcelona since its opening. It was the first commercial Spanish vermouth distillery. This same distillery also produces a Spanish absinthe—absenta—and wines.

PRODUCT: Vermouth Perucchi Gran Reserva Rojo

NOTES: A selection of wines are macerated with 40 botanicals to make this vermouth. The Spanish Table notes: "The red Vermouth has great complexity and flavors of christmas cookie spices, bitters, lemon, cola with lingering clove and spice. Just a hint of sweetness..." 15% ABV

PRODUCT: Vermouth Perucchi Gran Reserva Blanco

PROCESS: The Spanish Table notes: "The white Vermouth from Montana Perucchi is oustanding with notes of jasmine, honeysuckle, ginger and a touch of sassafras. Notes of spice and citrus peel and a lingering flavor that reminds me of biting into a soft, honey ginger cake with just a touch more sweetness than the red vermouth." 15% ABV

Montenegro S.r.l., Bologna, Italy

www.montenegro.it

This amaro was first produced by Stanislao Cobianchi, in 1885, and is named after Princess Elena of Montenegro on the occasion of her marriage to Italy's sovreign King Vittorio Emmanuel III.

Amaro Montenegro uses a blend of over 40 different herbs from all over the world. Amaro Montenegro uses a distinct soaking and distillation process which results in a sweet tasting liquor with a slightly bitter finish.

PRODUCT: Amaro Montenegro

NOTES: Over 40 botanicals are macerated in spirit to create this amaro. Wine Enthusiast notes: "Displays early botanical scents of orange peel, fresh not dried coriander, red cherry, pekoe tea and cucumber. Palate entry is sweet at first then it quickly turns mildly bitter and botanical; by midpalate, there's a slight sweetness of tangerine/mandarin peel. Aftertaste is moderately bittersweet and citrusy." 23% ABV

Nando, Italy

No company details are available at the time of this printing.

PRODUCTS: Nando Vermouth Dry, Nando Vermouth Sweet

Noilly Prat & Cie., Marseillan, France

www.noillyprat.com

Absinthe and liqueur maker Joseph Noilly developed the first French "dry" vermouth formula, in 1813, based on wines that are subjected to the heat and sea-air of coastal Languedoc-Roussillon. Noilly's son Louis took over the business, in 1829, renaming it Louis Noilly & Sons. Exportation of its absinthe, liqueurs, and vermouth outside of France commenced the following year. When Louis' brother-in-law Claudius Prat joined the firm, in 1843, it was renamed Noilly-Prat. The next year, the company shipped its products across the Atlantic to the United States. Business grew to such a point that the vermouth and absinthe bottling operations as well as the firm's management offices were moved to the city of

Marseilles while its liqueur production was moved to Lyon. The process used today to make this vermouth is virtually unchanged since the 1850s.

PRODUCT: Noilly Prat Original Dry Vermouth

NOTES: Noilly Prat is made exclusively from white grape varieties grown in the Marseillan area, principally Picpoul de Pinet and Clairette. These light, fruity wines which are matured in massive Canadian oak casks for 8 months inside the original storerooms. They are then transferred to smaller oak barrels which are taken outside and left for a year where they they are exposed to the sun, wind, and low winter temperatures. The result is a wine that is dry, full-bodied and amber coloured, similar to Madeira or Sherry.

Brought back inside and left to rest for a few months, the wines are then blended together into oak casks. A small quantity of mistelle (grape juice and alcohol) is added to the wines in order to soften them, along with a dash of fruit essence to accentuate their flavour.

Over the course of three weeks, a blend of some 20 botanicals is added by hand every day into the wine-filled oak casks. Chamomile, bitter orange peel, nutmeg, centaury, coriander, and cloves are just a few of the plants used in the recipe. After a further six weeks, the finished product is shipped in tankers to Beaucaire, Gard where it is bottled by Martini & Rossi. Floral and grapey, very assertive, full bodied, light straw, a hint of salt air, and a distinctly drying finish. Wine

Enthusiast notes: "Extremely pale yellow. Wonderfully alive in the nose, as subtle, woodsy scents of juniper, thyme and laurel make an impression. It's clean, dry and refreshing at palate entry; midpalate shows traces of citrus, pine and berries. Aftertaste is harmonious and medium-long." 18% ABV.

PRODUCT: Noilly Prat Rouge Vermouth

NOTES: This red vermouth is made in exactly the same way, but with the addition of 30 botanicals which, with the traditional addition of caramel, produce the rich red colour. It is not sold in France, except at the Noilly Prat shop in Marseillan, being produced for export, principally to the United States. Wine Enthusiast notes: "Nut-brown, this is tinged with pale green and a deep, sweet winy aroma. There is a full, slightly herbal flavor, with lingering dried fruit and Sherry notes. Medium body, mouth-coating feel."

PRODUCT: Noilly Prat Ambre Vermouth

NOTES: Created in 1986, it is still sometimes referred to at the distillery as "the baby" of the Noilly product family. This vermouth is only available at the Noilly Prat shop in Marseillan, though for a few years it was exported to England. Significant flavours include cardamom, cinnamon, and lavender. Reminiscent of an excellent marsala, it leads with dry apricot and raisins. It is silky in the mouth, and makes a superb dessert wine. 16% ABV.

Nonino Distillatori S.p.A., Percoto, Italy

www.nonino.it

Orazio Nonino opened this grappa distillery in 1897, in Ronchi di Percoto. By 1928, the family moved operations to Percoto.

PRODUCT: Amaro Quintessentia Amaro

NOTES: Made from an aqua vitae base of Ribolla, Traminer, and Verduzzo grapes that is aged for over 5 years in French oak and used sherry barrels, this amaro features wild alpine botanicals from Carnia. A very elegant, smooth bitter. 35% ABV

Paolucci Liquori International S.r.l., Sora, Italy

www.paolucciliquori.it

Paolucci Liquori was founded by Vincent Paolucci, in 1873, who was fascinated by the medicinal plants found in Italy's Ciociaria region and their extraction for liqueur production.

PRODUCT: Amaro CioCiaro

NOTES: Amaro CioCiaro is based on a traditional recipe from Italy's Ciociaro region. No tasting notes are available as of this printing. 30% ABV

PRODUCT: Fernet Paolucci

NOTES: The recipe was developed by Vincent's son, Donatto. No tasting notes are available as of this printing.

Petrus, The Netherlands

A bitter liqueur that was originally produced in Leidschendam, around 1780, this bitter liqueur was very popular in the Netherlands and Belgium. Amongst the many producers of this particular style are Hubert Underberg and Petrus.

PRODUCT: Petrus Boonekamp Liqueur

NOTES: Distilled from botanicals including galangal, this bitter liqueur is commonly served as a digestive. 45% ABV

Picon, Marseille, France

www.diageo.com

Gaétan Picon, born in 1809, apprenticed at distilleries in Aix-en-Provence, Toulon and Marseille. After his tour of duty with the French Army in Algeria, in 1837, he invented Picon, establishing a distllery to produce African bitters in an Algerian village. He went on to build three other distilleries: Constantine, Bône and Algiers. Picon returned to France, in 1872, and built the Marseille distillery, where Picon is still produced. During the 1970s, the strength of Picon was reduced to 25% ABV. In 1989, it was reduced yet again to 18% ABV, and remains at that strength today.

PRODUCT: Amer Picon Club Liqueur Bitters

NOTES: Picon is a caramel-coloured, flavoured bitters drunk as an apéritif, which traditionally accompanies beer in the east and north of France. It is made from a base of fresh oranges which are dried and mixed with a solution of alcohol that is distilled and then infused with gentian and quinquina in equal measures. Sugar, syrup and caramel are added last. 18% ABV

Quady Winery, Madera, California

www.vya.com

Andrew and Laurel Quady produced their first wine in 1975, making a port at Lodi Vintners in Amador County, California. In 1980, they added a fortified dessert wine to their production and another in 1983. The line, and the team continued to grow and in 1998, Vya Vermouth was launched.

PRODUCT: Vya Extra Dry Vermouth

NOTES: This American vermouth is well-rounded with hint of orange, chamomile, and ginger, but not as dry as European vermouths. The Beverage Testing Institute notes: "Pale golden color. Bright, spicy sandalwood, herbal bark, and mincemeat pie like aromas with a silky, dry-yet-fruity medium body and a tart cinnamon bark and stone fruit skin and pit accented finish. A very nicely balanced and robust white vermouth." 18% ABV

PRODUCT: Vya Sweet Vermouth

NOTES: A rich, full-flavoured sweet American vermouth made with a base of Orange Muscat wine (normally used in the production of dessert wine) and infused with botanicals. Beverage Testing Institute notes: "Reddish mahogany color. Dense aromas and flavor of cola nut, sassafras, molasses menthol and spices with a sweet medium body and a long, tangy, dried fruit and dusty spice driven finish." 16% ABV.

RO.DI.A. S.p.A., Torino, Italy

www.garroneitaly.com

A 20-year-old conglomerate based in Torino. No other company details are available at the time of this printing.

PRODUCT: Garrone Vermouth Bianco

NOTES: Strong character, full bodied with a delicate aroma. Finish is sweet and sour. 16% ABV

PRODUCT: Garrone Vermouth Rosso

NOTES: Full bodied, aromatic. Made with 30 botanicals. 16% ABV

PRODUCT: Garrone Vermouth Extra Dry

NOTES: Strong perfume and absence of sweetness. 16% ABV

Stock S.r.l., Trieste, Italy and Slovenia

www.stock-spa.it

www.stock.cz

Lionello Stock founded, in 1884, the Camis & Stock Company in Trieste, Italy, which was then part of the Austro-Hungarian Holy Roman Empire. The company produced brandies until the end of the First World War, then trade became difficult when countries of the empire were divided. Stock bought a distillery in Božkov, where spirits made in Trieste could be shipped and bottled.

Fernet Stock begin production at this facility in 1927, only to be hit by the the global economic downturn of the Great Depression. The facility was seized in 1939 during German occupation. After the Second World War. Lionello Stock briefly regained possession, in 1947, until all commercial properties were nationalized the following year.

PRODUCT: Radis Amaro di Erbe

NOTES: A product of Stock Trieste, aromatic botanicals are macerated in spirit prior to distillation to produce this amaro. Additional spirit plus sugar and caramel are added, resulting in a pleasantly soft bitter, rich in aromas.

PRODUCT: Stock Vermouths

NOTES: Lionello Stock's original recipe for Stock Vermouth is based on a combination of Italian table wine, fortified with Italian brandy, and more than 50 botanicals. Available as Extra Dry, Rosso or Bianco.

PRODUCT: Amero di Limoncè

NOTES: Amaro Limoncè is a dark herbal bitters with a profound infusion of Italian lemons more than 30 botanicals, including gentian, juniper, dittany, angelica, cinchona, thyme, and coriander in a spirit base.

PRODUCT: Fernet Stock

NOTES: An especially bitter blend of 14 botanicals infused in spirit and matured in both oak casks and enamelled tanks. It is among the most popular spirits in the Czech Republic.

PRODUCT: Fernet Stock Citrus

NOTES: A younger "brother" of Fernet Stock, it is a unique combination of citrus fruits and botanicals.

PRODUCT: Fernet Stock Z Generation

NOTES: Fernet Stock Z Generation is a new product innovation launched in 2011, that combines fernet botannicals with ginger and mango.

PRODUCT: Fernet Stock Exclusive

NOTES: Following the same recipe as Fernet Stock, but in this limited edition, the liquid is aged in small, Scotch whiskey barrels that once contained Scotch whisky.

Sutton Cellars, San Francisco, California

www.suttoncellars.com

Sutton Cellars was started, in 1996, by Carl Sutton who started by producing 350 cases of four handcrafted varietal wines. Introduced in 2009, the Sutton Cellars Brown Label is also made in small batches.

PRODUCT: Sutton Cellars Brown Label Vermouth

PROCESS: Neutral white wine fortified with unaged brandy, infused with 17 botanicals, blended, and bottled fresh weekly. 17% ABV

Toso S.p.A., Cassano Belbo, italy

www.toso.it

No company details are available as of this printing.

PRODUCT: Toso Vermouth Rosso

NOTES: A very dark colour and the nose of a classic red vermouth. Light and sweet, with hints of vanilla.14.8% ABV

PRODUCT: Toso Vermouth di Torino Bianco

NOTES: White sweet vermouth, pale golden colour beautifully infused with aromatic herbs. 14.8% ABV

PRODUCT: Toso Vermouth Extra Dry

NOTES: Pale yellow straw colour, delicate fragrant floral aroma with attractive aromatic herbal flavour. 14.8% ABV

PRODUCT: Toso Americano Rosso

NOTES: No tasting notes available at the time of this printing. 14.8% ABV

PRODUCT: Toso L'Orange Apertivo Mediterraneo Vermouth

NOTES: No tasting notes available at the time of this printing. 14.8% ABV

Tosti S.p.A., Canelli, Italy

tosti.kdevelop.net

John Bosca first started making wines in 1820 and in 1925 the family-owned company produced vermouth for export to Somalia and Ethiopia. But it was during the 1950s, when it began trade in the United States, the company changed its name to Tosti.

PRODUCT: Gibo Vermouth di Torino Rosso

NOTES: No tasting notes are available at the time of this printing. 15% ABV

PRODUCT: Gibo Extra Dry Vermouth

NOTES: No tasting notes are available at the time of this printing. 15% ABV

PRODUCT: Gibo Vermouth Bianco

NOTES: No tasting notes are available at the time of this printing. 15% ABV

PRODUCT: Gibo Aperitivo Americano

NOTES: No tasting notes are available at the time of this printing. 15% ABV

PRODUCT: Tosti Vermouth di Torino Rosso

NOTES: No tasting notes are available at the time of this printing. 15% ABV

PRODUCT: Tosti Vermouth Extra Dry

NOTES: Notes of cardamom, cinnamon, allspice, marjoram, and chamomile. 15% ABV

Valsa Nuevo Perlino S.p.A, Asti, Italy

www.perlino.com

No company details are available at the time of this printing.

PRODUCT: Casa Martelletti Vermouth Classico

NOTES: Moscato base. Ambre hue. Intense with aromatic herbs; very complex with distinct notes of vanilla, bitter orange, gentian, china and rhubarb, Sweet with exceptional body and a pleasant artemesia finish. 16% ABV

PRODUCT: Filipetti Vermouth Bianco

NOTES: Straw yellow. Well-balanced and intense with aromatic herbs and spices. Typically full and persistent taste. 15% ABV

PRODUCT: Filipetti Vermouth Rosso

NOTES: Amber. Well-balanced with aromatic herbs, spices and traces of vanilla Typically full and persistent. 15% ABV

PRODUCT: Filipetti Vermouth Dry

NOTES: Pale straw yellow. Bouquet of aromatic herbs and spices with a note of juniper. Typically dry and persistent. 15% ABV

PRODUCT: Perlino Vermouth di Torino Bianco

NOTES: Straw yellow. Maceration in alcohol of the aromatic herbs and spices for a minimum of 30 days, then blended with the wine and sugar. rested for 3 weeks before filtration and bottling. Well-balanced and intense with aromatic herbs, spices and a note of vanilla. Typically dry and persistent. 15% ABV

PRODUCT: Perlino Vermouth di Torino Rosso

NOTES: Amber. Maceration in alcohol of the aromatic herbs and spices for a minimum of 30 days, then blended with the wine and sugar. rested for 3 weeks before filtration and bottling. Well-balanced with aromatic herbs and spices. Typically dry and persistent. 15% ABV

PRODUCT: Perlino Vermouth Extra Dry

NOTES: Pale straw yellow. Maceration in alcohol of the aromatic herbs and spices for a minimum of 30 days, then blended with the wine and sugar. rested for 3 weeks before filtration and bottling. Bouquet of aromatic herbs and spices with a note of juniper. Typically dry and persistent. 15% ABV

PRODUCT: Filipetti Americano

NOTES: Brilliant ruby red. Intense bouquet, recalling oranges and armoatic herbs. Full and sweet taste with a slightly bitter finish. 16% ABV

PRODUCT: Fernet Franzini Amaro

NOTES: Made by the Franzini distillery since 1915. No tasting notes available at the time of this printing. 40% ABV

PRODUCT: Fernet-Menta Franzini Liquore

NOTES: Made by the Franzini distillery since 1915. No tasting notes available at the time of this printing. 40% ABV

Yzaguirre, El Morell, Spain

www.vermutyzaguirre.com

The Yzaguirre y Simó winery was founded in 1884 in Reus, Spain and has been producing dry wines, mistelas, and vermouths since its inception.

PRODUCT: Vermouth Rojo Yzaguirre

NOTES: Nose intense with notes of herbs and special touches Light balsamic aromatic structure we provide a pleasant and very particular. Good aromatic intensity on the palate, nicely balanced acidity with long and intense bitter aftertaste. 15% ABV

PRODUCT: Vermouth Rojo Reserva Estuchado Yzaguirre

NOTES: Initial taste in the mouth very alcoholic but in excellent condition with the acidity of the product. Glucose in high percentage, which offers a product velvety and mouth are nice wood notes, herbs and spices. One year in oak barrels help to stabilize the flavor and color of the mixture made. 18% ABV

PRODUCT: Vermouth Reserva Rojo Yzaguirre

NOTES: No tasting notes available at the time of this printing. 18% ABV

PRODUCT: Vermouth Blanco Yzaguirre

NOTES: No tasting notes available at the time of this printing. 15% ABV

PRODUCT: Vermouth Reserva Blanco Yzaguirre

NOTES: No tasting notes available at the time of this printing. 18% ABV

PRODUCT: Vermouth Extra Dry Yzaguirre

NOTES: No tasting notes available at the time of this printing. 18% ABV

Zucca, Milan, Italy

Ettore Zucca created this rhubarb-based amaro, in 1845, in Milano, where it became a staple amongst café society and was appreciated by the ducha House of Savoy House. The amaro lent its name to a famous Milanese café—the Zucca—which was opened in 1867 and still stands today at the Galleria's entrance, just opposite the Duomo. The same site was also the location where Gaspare Campari first introduced his bitters during the 1860s.

PRODUCT: Zucca

NOTES:Zucca is a bittersweet Italian amaro. Although 'Zucca' is the Italian word for squash / pumpkin, its base ingredient is rhubarb. Hence the name Zucca Rabarbaro. The recipe includes zest, cardamom seeds and other curative herbs. After 10 days of rest, the drink is filtered and bottled. 16% ABV

Zwack, Budapest, Hungary

www.zwack.hu

For two hundred years, the Zwack family has produced Unicum from a recipe developed by an ancestor who was royal physician to the Habsburg emperor. During the Socialist regime in Hungary, the Zwack family lived in exile in New York and Chicago: during this time, Unicum in Hungary was produced according to a different formula. However, before moving to America, Janos Zwack entrusted a family friend in Milan with the production of Unicum based on the original recipe. After the fall of communism, Péter Zwack returned to Hungary and resumed production of the original product.

PRODUCT: Unicum

NOTES: A portion of the 40 botanicals is macerated for 30 days, while the other part is distilled. Then both elements are blended together and aged in oak casks for a minimum of six months. The result is the national drink of Hungary.

PRODUCT: Zwack St Hubertus Herbal Liqueur

NOTES: Beverage Testing Institute notes: "Golden amber color. Rich aromas of honeyed herbal bark and roots and stewed cherries follow through to a round, sweet medium-to-full body with honeyed raisin and spice notes and a long, tangy candied tangerine peel, herb and cinnamon bark fade."

CHAPTER FIVE
SERVING VERMOUTH

Complexity and sophistication. Elegant, yet open to variation. That's the simplest definition we can offer as an introduction to the Vermouth Family of cocktails. When vermouth made its way from cafés as a straight up or on the rocks beverage to cocktail bars as an equal share partner to each of the major spirits categories, it evoked poetry, debate, literary prowess, and almost manic subjectivity as its use and execution. However, there has never been a debate as to what vermouth brings to a mixed drink: roundness and richness of flavour, accentuation of good spirits, a symphony of subtle bitter and sweet botanical notes. There is a reason vermouth has been such an enduring mixed drink ingredient. It is a perfect mixer and modifier for spirits. There is also a reason it fell out of favour and is now returning rapidly: it takes a bit of skill and understanding to mix with vermouth.

A few tips before we delve into the origins and the myriad of modern variations on these classic recipes. Think of these as six commandments for incorporating vermouth into your drinks repertoire.

1. Vermouth should always be used fresh. The botanicals and wine, while stabilized from further fermentation, do lose subtlety and complexity with oxidation over time.

2. Always refrigerate vermouth after opening to retard oxidation. It is a wine. It may be fortified and stouter of constitution than a beaujolais, but it is still a wine. It has less alcohol on average than port.

3. After months in the refrigerator, vermouth is still good for cooking but less so for drinking.

4. Vermouth is excellent for reducing the ABV of mixed drinks, for more responsible service, without detracting from a cocktail's strength of flavour.

5. Shaking a drink with vermouth causes it to cloud and foam slightly, while it intensifies the flavour. If you wish to create a clear Martini or Manhattan you should stir the drink. However, shaking will not damage the flavour, so there is nothing wrong with shaking a drink containing vermouth.

6. Half bottles are an excellent solution for keeping fresh vermouth on hand, iif you are not pouring enough to finish full bottles while they are still fresh. Minis, kept chilled in the vegetable crisper of your refrigerator, are even better. Unopened, and away from sun and intense heat, a bottle of vermouth will keep for years.

What can you say about a beverage that marries so well with other spirits? Throughout the course of drinks history, vermouth has proven itself as the ultimate companion.

GIN & VERMOUTH: THE MARTINI & ITS SIBLINGS

An anonymous writer said it best: "I'm not talking a cup of cheap gin splashed over an ice cube. I'm talking satin, fire, and ice. Fred Astaire in a glass. Surgical cleanliness. Insight and comfort. Redemption and absolution. I'm talking a Martini." This cocktail, the ultimate spotlight for the attributes of gin and vermouth, continues to elicit controversy and conversation around the globe.

The Martini had sweet beginnings, literally. Back in the 1880s when Italian and French vermouths landed in Britain and the United States in rapidly rising quantities, they were frequently paired with Old Tom gin, a lightly sweet style with a hint of licorice. Although its been bantered about that the Martinez was the Martini's parent, invented by Jerry "The Professor" Thomas, the famed mixologist did not include that drink nor the Martini in his seminal 1862 book *How to Mix Drinks or the Bon-Vivant's Companion*. It did, however, appear in the 1887 edition that was published after Thomas's death in 1885. The Martinez is an excellent drink and a close cousin, but there is no conclusive link.

(Much of the story was created by a San Francisco advertising agency in the 1960s.)

Who did publish the first Martini recipe? Amongst the half dozen vermouth plus spirit drinks Harry "The Dean" Johnson included his 1882 *The New and Improved Illustrated Bartenders' Manual* was the earliest and sweetest version.

MARTINI
30 ml Old Tom gin
30 ml Italian vermouth
2 or 3 dashes Boker's bitters
2 or 3 dashes gomme syrup
Stir over ice. Strain into a cocktail glass. Garnish with a cherry or a medium-sized olive. Squeeze a lemon twist on top.

Johnson also presented a simplified version, which he published in the same book, called the Bradford à la Martini.

BRADFORD À LA MARTINI
30 ml Old Tom gin
30 ml Italian vermouth
3 or 4 dashes orange bitters
Shake well over ice. Strain into a cocktail glass. Garnish with a medium-sized olive.

You're probably asking yourself why these two drinks were called Martini? The answer is shockingly simple. Even though Louis Noilly's "dry" vermouth was exported to Britain, beginning in 1830, and the United States in 1844, the drinking world was still in a sweet phase. Of the ten cocktail recipes in Jerry Thomas's 1862 book, none of them included vermouth—French or Italian.

Then, the first company to launch into large-scale commercial vermouth production and international marketing took the stage. The Sola family sold out its share of Martini, Sola & Cia, in 1879, and the company became known as Martini & Rossi. The popularity of this brand had already reached the point where café patrons simply asked for a glass of Martini when they wanted a glass of Vermouth di Torino or Italian vermouth. Between 1867 and 1889, the company exported 612,000 litres of its product to the US.

With Harry Johnson's book, the growing profession of mixology was introduced to a simple equation: spirit plus vermouth and a hint of bitters.

It wasn't the only time that a mixed drink was named after a brand. A few others have followed, such as the Bacardí Cocktail (a Daiquirí with a touch of grenadine syrup). But the Martini achieve the greatest and enduring fame.

Johnson played around with the balanced pairing of gin and vermouth again, adding Chartreuse as a third element in a symphony of botanical aromas and character that he called the Bijou.

BIJOU COCKTAIL
20 ml Chartreuse Vert
20 ml Italian vermouth

20 ml Plymouth gin
1 dash orange bitters
Stir and strain into a chilled cocktail glass. Garnish with a cherry or
medium-size olive. Squeeze a piece of lemon peel on top and serve.

The dryness of French vermouth also captured his imagination when he created the Tuxedo Cocktail.

TUXEDO COCKTAIL
1 or 2 dashes maraschino liqueur
1 dash absinthe
2 or 3 dashes orange bitters
30 ml French vermouth
30 ml Sir Burnett's Tom gin
Stir and strain into a chilled cocktail glass. Garnish with a cherry.
Squeeze a piece of lemon peel on top and serve.

Johnson also opened the way to the cocktail's drier future with his presentation of the mother of the modern-day Martini, the Marguerite Cocktail.

MARGUERITE COCKTAIL
30 ml Plymouth Dry Gin
30 ml French vermouth
2 or 3 dashes orange bitters
2 or 3 dashes anisette
Stir over ice. Strain into a cocktail glass. Garnish with a
cherry and squeeze a lemon twist on top.

The Marguerite Cocktail seemed to strike a chord with American drinkers. Streamlined and dried even further--in keeping with a trend at that time away from sweet drinks-- when Thomas Stuart published his 1896 book *Stuart's Fancy Drinks and How to Mix Them*, where it was featured in the "New and Up-to-Date Drinks" section. The drink was a symphony of simplicity.

MARGUERITE COCKTAIL
1 dash orange bitters
40 ml Plymouth gin
20 ml French vermouth
Stir over ice. Strain into a cocktail glass. Garnish with a cherry and
squeeze a lemon twist on top.

The following year, another name for this drink appeared in *The New York Journal* as the Alaska Gold Rush was in full swing: "The Klondike Cocktail has made its appearance in a dozen first class bars downtown. It is made preferably of gin, with vermouth and orange bitters—really along the lines of the Martini, but the 'Klondike suggestion' is given by a floating piece of lemon or orange peel cut into a disk and just the size of a $20 gold piece."

The obvious high demand for this dry Martini was answered by Martini & Rossi with its 1890 introduction of Martini Extra Dry vermouth. These clever early cocktail names were quickly forgotten and the term Martini finally welded itself to this drink when the company's American importer G.F. Heublein & Brothers got on the cocktail bandwagon with its launch of Heublein Club Cocktails, the world's first commercial line of pre-mixed, bottled cocktails. Naturally, one of the first offerings was the Martini Cocktail (Heublein also offered a drink called a Vermouth Cocktail which contained no gin). Of the 14,715,564 litres of Martini & Rossi's vermouth exported to the US, 308,713 litres alone were devoted to this bottled cocktail partnership.

A custody battle ensued. Three establishments claimed that they gave birth to the Dry Martini: The American Bar at London's Savoy Hotel, Manhattan's Knickerbocker Hotel in the hands of Martini di Arma di Taggia, and Signor Martinez at Manhattan's Waldorf-Astoria Hotel.

Then personal preference became part of the Martini's mystique before and after the First World War as cocktails flowed on both sides of the Atlantic Ocean. While Americans were in the throes of Prohibition, the British took their turn at refining the Silver Bullet as evidenced in Robert de Fleury's 1934 book *1700 Cocktails for the Man Behind the Bar*. Five Martini recipes were documented, ranging from an Old Tom with Italian; a London dry with Italian; a London dry with dry French; a Plymouth dry with both Italian and French; to a London dry with Italian and a hint of apéritif wine.

The Martini went bone dry when Nazi forces occupied France and Italy, bringing vermouth exports to a virtual standstill. Confronted with open bottles that were months old, aficionados passed the soured vermouth bottle over the shaker instead of pouring in a single drop. Diehards such as British Field Marshal Bernard Montgomery reconfigured the ratio to 12 parts gin to 1 part vermouth.

Creator of the James Bond spy novels, Ian Fleming was a well-heeled, black sheep of an aristocratic family. After failing his foreign service exams he tried to follow in his illustrious brother Peter's footsteps writing for Reuters News Service. No fortune to be made there. So he dabbled in banking before landing a post with naval intelligence just as Britain declared war on Germany. The seeds of his inspiration were sown during those war-torn years.

Fellow Etonian and part-owner of the North American Newspaper Alliance, Ivar Bryce invited Fleming to Jamaica to attend a naval conference on Nazi U boat warfare in the Caribbean and to visit his own estate. The serenity of the tropical landscape was a stark contrast to the war-ravaged urban rubble of London: Lush fruits and bountiful fish instead of ration books and food shortages. Spirits that flowed like water. It was too much for an uncompromising, hard drinking, heavy smoking aristocrat to resist. He built Goldeneye, an unpretentious winter escape from London life and his work as a reporter for Kemsley Newspapers Limited. There, from January through March, he basked in the island's beauty when he wasn't womanising or gambling.

All of that changed when Fleming found himself waiting at Goldeneye for his pregnant, long-time mistress Lady Anne Rothemere to finalise her divorce. On 17 February 1952, he sat at his desk and began first draft of his novel *Casino Royale*, which introduced the super-spy character James Bond.

Published in 1953, Fleming described the contents and execution of his perfect "violet hour" libation:

> "A dry martini," he said. "One. In a deep champagne goblet."
> "Oui, monsieur."
> "Just a moment. Three measures of Gordon's, one of vodka, half a measure of Kina Lillet. Shake it very well until it's ice-cold, then add a large thin slice of lemon-peel. Got it?"

Through the guise of James Bond, Fleming justified this recipe by adding: "I never have more than one drink before dinner. But I do like that one to be large and very strong and very cold and very well-made. I hate small portions of anything, particularly when they taste bad. This drink's my own invention. I'm going to patent it when I can think of a good name."

By the time author Ian Fleming and his superspy character James Bond firmly posited the Martini into the psyches of 1950s drinkers, the 3-to-1 Dry Martini was the standard by which people adhered until the Martini all but disappeared during the short hiatus in which Seventies sippers lived on long drinks and wine spritzers because the Martini was their parents' call.

DRY MARTINI
45 ml Beefeater London Dry Gin
15 ml French vermouth
Stir or shake over ice. Strain into a cocktail glass. Garnish with an olive or lemon twist.

You can thank Generation X for rediscovering classic bars, classic cocktails, and cocktail culture. The mid-1990s saw a whole new audience of drinkers and mixers reviving the debate over proportions, mixing styles, types of gin, and styles of vermouth. Nearly two decades later, you can walk into any bar in the world and find yourself face to face with a different variation on the Martini.

Audrey Saunders of Pegu Club in New York favours a Fifty-Fifty. Dushan Zaric of Employees Only and Macao Trading Company prefers a 3-to-1 Beefeater Martini. Alessandro Palazzi at Duke's Hotel in London serves up a mere mist of vermouth in his frozen Plymouth Gin version. See what we mean?

So what's the best way to approach the making and drinking of this ultimate classic? In his 1948 book *The Hour*, author Bernard De Voto said it best: "We may understand how cults form with the Martini as with all arts, how rituals develop, how superstitions and even sorcerous beliefs and practices betray a faith that is passionate and pure but runs easily into fanaticism. But though we understand these matters we must not be lenient toward them for they divide fellowship."

The Martini wasn't the only drink to touch the hearts of American sippers.

WHISKEY/WHISKY & VERMOUTH: THE MANHATTAN & ITS SIBLINGS

The Manhattan Cocktail may or may not have been born at the Manhattan Club when it was at Fifth Avenue and 34th Street in New York City, but there is no doubt it was popularized there (though not, as legend would have it, by Manhattan socialite Jenny Jerome—she was at Blenheim Palace in the UK for her son Winston Churchill's birth and christening at the time she supposedly invented it). When the club published a 50th anniversary book for its members in 1915, they included their secret recipe and staked their claim that they had given birth to the world's most popular whiskey drink when the club opened in the 1860s.

MANHATTAN COCKTAIL
30 ml bourbon whiskey

30 ml Italian vermouth
2 dashes orange bitters
Combine ingredients in an ice-filled mixing glass and stir until chilled (about 20 seconds). Strain into a chilled cocktail glass. Note: garnish was out of fashion when the drink was born, but you can add an orange twist. Why orange bitters? Angostura was not imported to New York until after the drink was born.

Harry Johnson added a couple of flourishes to his 1882 version, adding a dash of gomme syrup and a dash of curaçao or absinthe, topped with a lemon twist.

In a mere 30 years the recipe got a little sweeter and spicier with the introduction of Angostura bitters as a replacement for orange bitters. One of the most famous bartenders of that era was Willie "The Only William" Schmidt, whose bar once stood on the spot that is now more or less precisely the center-point of ground zero at the World Trade Center in New York. His 1891 recipe demonstrated the shift in public preference.

MANHATTAN COCKTAIL
40 ml bourbon whiskey
20 ml Italian vermouth
2 dashes of bitters
2 dashes of gomme (simple) syrup
Combine ingredients in an ice-filled mixing glass. Stir. Strain into a chilled cocktail glass. Optional: a few dashes of maraschino liqueur.

American whiskeys were not the only spirit in the category to join the Vermouth Family. Blended scotch whisky made its entry into the growing American spirits market in the late 1890s. Usher's Old Vatted Glenlivet, Dewar's White Label, Chivas' Royal Strathythan were shipping hundreds of thousands of cases to the US. Whisky made the headlines more than once in that decade. Industrial magnate Andrew Carnegie, the "Laird of Cluny Castle", made quite a stir, in 1890, when he ordered a barrel of scotch whisky to be imported and delivered to US President Benjamin J Harrison.

The world's first motion picture commercial was produced and displayed, in 1897, high above Herald Square in Manhattan. The subject? DEWAR'S SCOTCH WHISKY.

In December 1894, music critic and comic opera composer Reginald De Koven premiered his operetta *Rob Roy* on Broadway. Much in the style of Gilbert & Sullivan, De Koven's work often spun off into hit songs of the day. Such was the case with Rob Roy's "Dearest of My Heart" and "My Home Is Where the Heather Blooms".

The pairing of blended whisky's fanfared arrival and De Koven's operetta obviously struck a chord in Manhattan. Since the Manhattan and the Martini were the fashionable calls throughout the city, it's no surprise that the Rob Roy joined the ranks of sophisticated classics.

ROB ROY
30 ml blended scotch whisky
30 ml Italian vermouth
1 dash Angostura bitters
Shake ingredients over ice. Strain into a chilled cocktail glass.

Hugo R Ensslin, creator of the Aviation, provided a "perfect" version of the Rob Roy a decade later while working at the Hotel Wallick in Manhattan. Called the Affinity, it adds a touch more spice and dryness.

AFFINITY
15 ml sweet vermouth
15 ml dry vermouth
30 ml blended scotch whisky
2 dashes Angostura bitters
Stir ingredients over ice. Strain into a chilled cocktail glass. Garnish with a lemon twist

Another drink that owes its name to the overwhelming success of a play, a song, or a book is the *Trilby*. Written by George du Maurier and published in 1894, Trilby tells the story of a tone-deaf girl who works as an artist's model and laundress in Paris who is transformed by the hypnotist Svengali into an operatic diva. A triangle forms when a young artist also falls in love with her.

The novel struck a chord that sang for decades. Its popularity at the turn of the century ran second only to Bram Stoker's 1897 novel *Dracula*.

Trilby inspired Gaston Leroux to write the 1910 novel *The Phantom of the Opera* which also spun over into an equally successful play that was revived numerous times into the 1920s. (The Trilby hat was an indirect spinoff of the play, in which one of the characters sported this narrow style of brim.)

Obviously, de Maurier's novel also chimed the right chord with Harry Johnson, who published a recipe for the Trilby in the 1900 edition of his *Bartenders' Manual*.

TRILBY COCKTAIL
2 dashes absinthe
2-3 dashes orange bitters
2-3 dashes Parfait d'Amour
30 ml blended scotch whisky
30 ml Italian vermouth
Stir ingredients over ice. Strain into a chilled cocktail glass. Garnish with maraschino cherries and a lemon peel.

Parfait d'Amour—a violet-hued liqueur with citrus, almond, rose petal and vanilla notes—is an ingredient that appears in a few pre-Prohibition recipes. Like Crème de Violette and Créme de Noyau, this ingredient was dropped from the recipe by most American bartenders during the 1930s. Was it because importation was too costly? Or was it because drink recipes became much simpler in the years leading up to the Second World War?

Either way, the drink was streamlined by the time it appeared in the 1935 *Old Mr Boston Guide*:

TRILBY

30 ml blended scotch whisky

15 ml Italian vermouth

2 dashes orange bitters

Shake all ingredients over ice. Strain into a chilled cocktail glass.

Over in Britain, Harry Craddock was shaking up the cocktail world when he took over from Ada Coleman as head bartender at the Savoy's American Bar. First, he paid homage, in 1922, to Rudolph Valentino's box office hit, *Blood & Sand*, by crafting a delightfully smoky and zesty cocktail with the same name.

BLOOD & SAND

30 ml Chivas Regal

30 ml blood orange juice (sanguinello juice)

20 ml Italian vermouth

20 ml Cherry Heering

Shake all ingredients over ice. Strain into a chilled cocktail glass.

Flame an orange twist over the glass.

A few decades later, Joe Gilmore took Craddock's post at the Savoy, in 1955, serving such notables as George Bernard Shaw, Agatha Christie, Charlie Chaplin, and Sir Winston Churchill. A frequent parton of the American Bar, the former prime minister was honoured with more than one

Gilmore-divined drink that was customized to his tastes. A Whisky Sour with a spicy twist, the Churchill also suits Manhattan lovers.

CHURCHILL
60 ml Chivas Regal
20 ml fresh lime juice
20 ml Italian vermouth
20 ml Cointreau
Shake all ingredients over ice. Strain into a chilled cocktail glass.

When one talks of rum, the conversation usually leads to sweet drinks or sours: the Mojito, the Daiquirí, Piña Colada, Mai Tai. However, during vermouth's heydays, an elegant vermouth drink appeared in Havana, Cuba.

RUM & VERMOUTH: EL PRESIDENTE & ITS SIBLINGS

You could call it the Rum Manhattan. El Presidente, when it is mixed properly stands proudly alongside the Martini and the Manhattan—a sophisticated drink more suited to a jacket-required Havana nightclub than a sandy beachside bar. This is the sort of drink that pairs nicely with a good cigar, and holds its own before a steak (or roast suckling pig).

In 1928, British playwright and journalist Basil Woon published the most colourful portrait of Prohibition-era Havana entitled *When It's Cocktail Time in Cuba*. In this meaty volume, he detailed his encounters in the island country's casinos, country clubs, and naturally its cocktail bars.

He cited the Daiquirí as the most popular refreshment of the "earnest drinkers of Havana". Yet despite his detailed account of its compounding, Woon said another drink was "the aristocrat of cocktails and is the one preferred by the better class of Cubans". That drink is the El Presidente. And as with the Daiquirí, he documented El Presidente's recipe.

EL PRESIDENTE
30 ml Cuban silver rum
30 ml French vermouth
Dash of grenadine or curaçao
Shake ingredients over ice and strain into a chilled cocktail glass.
Garnish with an orange peel.

Where was this cocktail born? "The Sevilla-Biltmore is to Havana what the Ritz is to Paris, headquarters of the wealthy pleasure seeker," Woon proclaimed. Twice daily, the Old-Timers' Club—an informal gathering of prominent ex-pats and businessmen—gathered to share the creations of Eddie Woelke and Fred Kaufman. Across the hotel's long mahogany bar, Kaufman mixed a variety of original creations that featured pineapple juice. His most notable creation, of course, was the Mary Pickford (this drink is frequently miscredited to Woelke). Woelke was famed for his Mint Juleps that Woon swore would cause "any Southern gentleman to yelp the rebel yell."

Born in Philadelphia in 1877, Eddie had worked his way up to some of the world's finest watering holes. From the Germantown Cricket Club in his hometown he made his way to the Plaza Athenée in Paris, where he also met his wife. Returning to the US, he presided in 1906 at New York's Knickerbocker Hotel with a young Harry Craddock (of Savoy Hotel fame) at his side and then at the New York Biltmore when it opened seven years later. And with a stroke of great luck, he was invited in 1919 by its owners to be part of the opening team at their new property, Havana's Sevilla-Biltmore Hotel on Calle Trocadero.

General Mario García Menocal y Deop had been Cuba's president since his election in 20 May 1913. He was still in office when the hotel welcomed dignitaries, celebrities, and masters of industry visited this crown jewel of hospitality. Is it possible that Eddie put this drink on the menu to honour a visit from El Presidente? We may never know for sure. But popular lore has frequently noted that this was the politician's favourite recipe before he was voted out of office two years later.

Eddie moved on to the Casino National in 1924 (and some people say he also did a stint at the Havana American Jockey Club) when the Sevilla-Biltmore was closed for renovation. Who knows if he was responsible? But when President Gerardo Machado was voted into office the following year, El Presidente was slightly modified and renamed Presidente Machado.

A slim volume titled *El Arte de Hacer un Cocktail y Algo Mas* was published in Havana in 1927 by the Compañia Cervecera International S.A. There we find Eddie's Presidente as well as a Presidente Machado! What's the difference? Dashes of both grenadine and curaçao are used to enhance the marriage of rum and dry vermouth.

PRESIDENTE MACHADO
30 ml Cuban silver rum
30 ml French vermouth
Dash of grenadine
Dash of curaçao
Shake ingredients over ice and strain into a chilled cocktail glass.
Garnish with an orange peel.

We know that Machado was proud enough of his version to present it to another dignitary: Calvin Coolidge, who was US President during the height of Prohibition. An item appeared in the 17 January 1928 edition of *The Evening Independent* that noted that "although the state dinner given by President Machado of Cuba at the presidential palace last night in honor of President Coolidge was exceedingly wet, starting with a fiery 'presidente cocktail' and ending with fine old 1811 brandy, guests at the dinner insisted that President Coolidge did not drink any of the wines or liquors." American newspapermen at the scene tried to pry more details from guests and officials but none were forthcoming, so they declared without witnessing the dinner that Coolidge had scrupulously abstained.

El Presidente's and Presidente Machado's popularity continued in Havana's bars even after the Cuban president was exiled in 1933. Charles H Baker discovered it at Bar La Florida later in the decade. Constante Ribaligua Vert preferred to have his staff garnish it with a cocktail cherry. The Cuban bartenders' guild took a slight step back to Woelke's recipe and a baby step forward when they standardized recipe in their 1945 edition of *El Arte del Cantinero*.

PRESIDENTE
30 ml Cuban silver rum
30 ml French vermouth
Dash of grenadine
Shake ingredients over ice and strain into a chilled cocktail glass.
Garnish with an orange peel and a cocktail cherry.

Maybe it's because the public's palette for rum drinks ran to the sweet side with the rise of tiki during the 1940s, but El Presidente found himself shunted aside while the world clamoured for Donn Beach's and Trader Vic's night and day versions of the Mai Tai. The Puerto Rican Piña Colada with its creamy, coconut and pineapple thickness was a Sixties staple as were sweet, frozen incarnations of the Daiquirí.

Thankfully, the recent classic cocktail revival returned El Presidente to his rightful, aristocratic position—a showcase for the more refined characteristics of Cuban rum. If you are fortunate enough to spend a few quality hours and days in Havana, you can discover the beauty of sipping El Presidente while nestled into a thickly-cushioned wicker chair on the Hotel Nacional's tranquil veranda.

Notions for a Perfect Presidente appeared in 1992 at Victor's Café in Miami around 1992. The balance leaned more the spirit than the vermouth.

VICTOR'S EL PRESIDENTE
45 ml Cuban silver rum
25 ml Italian sweet vermouth
15 ml French dry vermouth
1 tsp grendaine
Shake ingredients over ice. Strain into a chilled cocktail glass. Garnish with a cocktail cherry.

Another New World spirit, tequila, also had its moment with vermouth.

TEQUILA & VERMOUTH: BOTH PERFECT & DRY

Not in the US or in Mexico, but in Britain is where tequila and vermouth met whilst the Bright Young People frollicked until all hours throughout London. Before the curtain drew on the devil may care era between 1920 and 1939, the British bartending profession should its might and muscle, forming the United Kingdom Bartenders Guild, the first of its kind. And then one of its presidents, William J Tarling, published a compendium of what London barmen were serving in the 1937 *Café Royal Cocktail Book.* One of the first cocktail books to offer up tequila based drinks, the Matador and Sombrero joined the Vermouth Family.

MATADOR
20 ml curaçao
20 ml French vermouth
20 ml silver tequila

SOMBRERO
20 ml Italian vermouth
20 ml French vermouth
40 ml silver tequila
Shake and strain into a chilled cocktail glass. Squeeze a lemon peel
on top.

COGNAC & VERMOUTH: SWEET MEMORY

The oaky dimensions of cognac work well with the bitter sweet aspects of vermouth and so foreign news correspondent Albert Stevens Crockett believed when he wrote his 1931 book *Old Waldorf Bar Days*. Prohibition in the US was on its last legs and Crockett's book paid homage to the cocktail's golden age, reminding readers of the joys of social sipping in the world's finest establishments. A drink that he "attributed to a once well-known and somewhat lively hotel, whose bar was long a center of life after dark in the Times Square district" was the Metropole.

METROPOLE
1 dash Peychaud Bitters
1 dash orange bitters
30 ml French vermouth
30 ml cognac or brandy
Stir and strain into a chilled cocktail glass. Garnish with a cherry.

SHERRY & VERMOUTH: HOMAGE TO A HIT

The rich allure of Spanish sherry has also served to be an ideal match to vermouth. Again, in Crockett's homage to bartending pre-Prohibition past, he noted a drink that was named after Edward Everett Rice's 1894 Broadway hit,

Adonis, which starred Henry E Dixey, one of the era's most popular performers.

ADONIS
2 dashes orange bitters
30 ml sherry
30 ml Italian vermouth
Stir and strain into a chilled cocktail glass.

BITTER APÉRITIF & VERMOUTH: THE PRODIGAL SON RETURNS

Bitter apéritifs such as Campari and vermouth have had a longstanding relationship that has made it the most common call at aperitivo. Legend has it that Gaspari Campari tried his hand at making an American-style cocktail around 1856 while working at Pasticceria Bass and the Ristorante del Cambio in Torino, adding soda water and a couple of lumps of ice to a glass of sweet vermouth. All the while Campari spent his off hours developing his bitter apéritif that combined 60 different herbs, spices, and fruits, plus a vibrant red colorant called "cochineal crimson E120."

He introduced his bitters, in 1860, into his American-style apéritif. It met with such rave reviews that Campari launched commercial production of his bitters in Milan. Two years later, Campari permanently settled in Milan and opened his own café where he served his signature drink, dubbed the Torino-Milano.

TORINO-MILANO
30 ml Campari bitter
30 ml Italian vermouth
Build ingredients in a rocks glass filled with ice. Top with soda water
and garnish with a slice of lemon.

While the economy was on the rise and travel was easy and cheap at the turn of the century, Americans exerted their influence on drinks around the world. Take for example the Torino-Milano. It was renamed "Americano" because locals noticed it was a favourite among American tourists.

But it took an ex-pat to elevate the drink to level of a true classic: Count Camillo Negroni, who returned, in 1920, from America to his native Italy. The young Negroni had been a cowboy in the American west and a gambler in New York during the nearly three decades Since the 29-year-old Milanese boarded the Fulda, on 16 May 1892, sailing from Genoa to New York in cabin accommodations. When Prohibition was enacted, Negroni returned to Firenze [Florence]. He frequented Caffé Casoni at Hotel Baglioni, where Fosco "Gloomy" Scarselli was famed for his Torino-Milanos (then called Americanos). One day Negroni asked for his Americano to be made without soda water. Instead he wanted gin. The Negroni was born. Negroni's Americano has the added kick of gin: a palate preference more in tune with American tastes.

NEGRONI
30 ml London dry gin
30 ml Campari
30 ml Italian vermouth
Shake with ice. Strain into a cocktail glass, or over ice in a tumbler.
Garnish with an orange twist.

A sparkling variation, Negroni Sbagliato, was invented during the 1950s at Bar Basso in Milano. A bartender was mixing a Negroni for an attractive female customer and accidentally substituted prosecco for the gin. While we question the story of this drink's birth (it would be much easier to mistake Prosecco for sparkling water than gin), there is no question this is an excellent aperitif. If you include the gin as well, it becomes an even better one.

NEGRONI SBAGLIATO
60 ml Prosecco
30 ml Campari
30 ml Italian vermouth
Shake with ice. Strain into a cocktail glass, or over ice in a tumbler.
Garnish with an orange twist.

If bitter apéritifs work with vermouth, what about their closest relations—amaros? There's one recipe that proves the equation works to a tee.

AMARO & VERMOUTH: A BIT OF HANK-PANKY

After he made his reputation throughout France, famed French chef Georges Auguste Escoffier and hotel manager César Ritz, in 1890, opened Richard D'Oyly Carte's Savoy Hotel on the Strand. (D'Oyly Carte made a fortune producing the operettas of W S Gilbert and Arthur Sullivan as well as owning the Savoy Theatre on the Strand.) When the Savoy reopened after its retrofit, in 1898, it sported an American bar with Frank Wells as its first head barman, according to former Savoy barmen Peter Dorelli and Joe Gilmore.

D'Oyly Carte also purchased Claridge's Hotel, in 1893, and commissioned the designer of Harrod's department store, C W Stephens, to rebuild the hotel from the ground up. Reopening, in 1898, it also featured an American bar in its renovation. But it also possessed a very unusual touch: a female bartender named Ada Coleman. According to historian Gary Regan, Coleman's father was a steward at the London golf club where D'Oyly Carte regularly played after he was introduced to the sport by baritone Rutland Barrington, who started in many Savoy productions.

When Ada's father passed away, a club member (possibly Richard D'Oyly Carte himself) gave the young woman a job as a bartender at Claridge's. She honed her craft there until 1903. Then, Rupert offered her the head bartender position at the Savoy. (D'Oyly Carte took over his father's seat as hotel chairman and opera company director two years earlier when the great impresario and entrepreneur passed away.)

"Coley", as she was affectionately called, served the hotel's celebrity-royalty driven roster which included Mark Twain, Prince William of Sweden, and actor-producer Sir Charles Henry Hawtrey, who named one of Coley's creations: the Hanky-Panky Cocktail.

HANKY-PANKY COCKTAIL
2 dashes Fernet Branca
30 ml Italian vermouth
30 ml London dry gin
Shake well and strain into cocktail glass. Squeeze orange peel on top.

In a 1925 edition of *The People* magazine, Coleman herself recalled: "The late Charles Hawtrey ... was one of the best judges of cocktails that I knew. Some years ago, when he was overworking, he used to come into the bar and say, 'Coley, I am tired. Give me something with a bit of punch in it.' It was for him that I spent hours experimenting until I had invented a new cocktail. The next time he came in, I told him I had a new drink for him. He sipped it, and, draining the glass, he said, 'By Jove! That is the real hanky-panky!' And Hanky-Panky it has been called ever since."

There is one last pairing that cannot be overlooked. You call it the ultimate union of sweet and dry, of bitter and smooth, of French and Italian vermouths.

VERMOUTH & VERMOUTH: SUCH LOVELY MUSIC

New York's Knickerbocker Hotel at Broadway and 42nd Street quickly became the hot spot for the rich and famous when it opened in 1906. Hotel resident Enrico Caruso and capitalist heir Harry Payne Whitney paid their respects at the lavishly-carved hotel bar that was presided by few celebrity mixologists of the day: Eddie Woelke, Adam Heiselman, and Harry Craddock.

According to Savoy legend Peter Dorelli's findings in the UKBG newsletters from the 1930s, the young Craddock worked his way from the Hollenden Hotel in Cleveland, Ohio, in 1892, to the Palmer House in Chicago the following year, before taking his post at Manhattan cocktailian hang-out, Hoffman House Hotel: all before joining the esteemed staff at the Knickerbocker.

This move might be explained by the movements of another New York bartender, James B Regan. Who? Haven't heard of him? Well, he didn't write a cocktail book, which is what gave virtually every bartender remembered today his fame. But Mr Regan should not be forgotten. As a shoeless boy on the oyster banks of New Jersey, he stood with his father gazing at Manhattan. His father said to him, "I give you all of that—to make good in."

Regan found a bar boy job in the old Earle's Hotel on Canal Street, squeezing lemons. He became a bartender at the Hoffman House Hotel. He became part-owner of the Pabst rathskeller, which stood on 42nd Street between Broadway and Seventh Avenue (the spot where the ball drops every New Year's Eve). He made the acquaintance of so many wealthy businessmen that when he decided to open his own bar, he simply turned to his best customers to find investors. After a few successful years as proprietor of the Woodmansten Inn in the Bronx, he received an invitation to return to Manhattan. One of his customers, John Jacob Astor was opening a new hotel and proposed that he manage it. On his way to becoming a multi-millionaire himself, Regan went a step further, taking on the Knickerbocker's lease. And he brought old colleagues like Craddock to work there, which brings us back to Harry.

When Prohibition took hold, Harry was fortunate that the world had remarkably efficient transatlantic transportation systems that allowed him to take his craft elsewhere. Harry fulfilled Jerry Thomas's dream of taking Europe by the scuff and teaching its citizens how to make and consume cocktails. (Plus, he still had the patronage of people like Jimmie Regan, who left "dry" America and bought himself a mansion near the American Ambassador in London.)

Harry Craddock arrived in Great Britain on 27 April 1920 in Liverpool with his wife and 16 year-old daughter, Lulu. It was no bed of roses for Harry. There was no fanfare when he arrived in London. An editorial comment appeared in a 1920 edition of *Catering Industry Employee:*

> "THE COCKTAIL IN LONDON. It is said that the cocktail offensive in London has failed, that the Englishman still sticks to the supping of his whisky and soda, instead of dashing off the 'dum-dum' of gin and vermouth. Perhaps the advance of the cocktail has been checked in London. That great American exile among potations may not yet have broken through the phlegm of the Englishman. But the check is only temporary."

Another items appears in the same publication:

> "London, Aug 31—(Special Cable)—'The Englishman prefers to sip his whisky and soda, not to toss it off quickly. For that reason he does not take to cocktails.' So said Harry Craddock, late of New York, now of London, who, last night, issued an official statement admitting defeat in his drive to substitute cocktails for the English drink. He had 200 cocktails on his wine list, but most of his patrons are Americans."

This didn't stop Craddock from campaigning for the cocktail's honour and, in 1923, he replaced the famed Ada Coleman at the Savoy. A 20 March 1923 notice on the International News Service read: "The cocktail season is about to open and Harry Craddock the 'cocktail king' has gone into training." The item went on to say that Craddock boasted of mixing at least 100,000 cocktails for the Savoy's American guests and a few thousand more for "visitors of other nationalities." Apparently, Craddock went into training at least two weeks before the season, working out at the gym for three hours in the morning and three hours in the afternoon just so he could be in peak condition.

He wasn't the only one taking exercise. The next year, it was noted that:

> "The new Lord Mayor of London is undergoing a tremendous ordeal. For the first eight weeks of his administration there is not a single day on which he has neither a banquet or a luncheon engagement. To offset this his physicians have ordered that he shall exercise daily . . . Although the Lord Mayor is himself a wine merchant, occasionally on his daily walk he slips into the Thames Embankment entrance of the Savoy to sample one of Harry Craddock's American cocktails."

A founding president of the United Kingdom Bartenders Guild, Craddock inscribed his name into cocktail history when, in 1930, he published *The Savoy Cocktail Book*. The be all, end all bible of British bartending well into the current century, Craddock knew how to work with vermouths. And within the first pages of his seminal tome, he presented the Addington.

ADDINGTON
30 ml French vermouth
30 ml Italian vermouth
Shake and strain into a chilled cocktail glass. Top with soda water and squeeze an orange peel on top.

But then, Harry Johnson has the last word on vermouth cocktails when he presented the Vermouth Cocktail in his 1882 *Bartenders' Manual*.

VERMOUTH COCKTAIL.
4 dashes gomme syrup
3 dashes Angostura bitters
60 ml Italian vermouth;
2 dashes maraschino liqueur
Stir ingredients over ice. Strain into a chilled cocktail glass. Twist a piece of lemon peel on top. And garnish with a cherry.

How could it be any simpler! Now it's time to create your own contribution to cocktail history.

INDEX

Inforamtion to come in the final edition.

CPSIA information can be obtained at www.ICGtesting.com
Printed in the USA
237944LV00002B/1/P